VERSES

FROM THE

HARVARD ADVOCATE.

Quattuordecim natus annos Græcam tragœdiam scripsi.
Qualem? inquis. Nescio: tragœdia vocabatur.
C. Plini Epistulæ.

CHARLES W. SEVER,
University Bookstore,
CAMBRIDGE.
1876.

Copyright,
By HURD AND HOUGHTON.
1876.

The Riverside Press, Cambridge:
Printed by H. O. Houghton and Company.

To

THE FOUNDERS OF THE ADVOCATE,

THE CLASS OF '67.

PREFACE.

THE "Harvard Advocate" was first published ten years ago. The following verses, selected from its twenty volumes, are not offered to the public on account of any excellence they may exhibit, or of any promise they may give, but because of such interest as they may have as a reflection of the thought and sentiment of the College, partly under the conditions which exist to-day and partly under those which are now rapidly disappearing. Their authors at the time of writing were, with one exception, we believe, either undergraduates or graduates whose separation from college had been so recent as not yet to break the ties they had formed as contributors to the "Advocate."

HARVARD COLLEGE, *May*, 1876.

CONTENTS.

PART I.

PART II.

PARAPHRASES, TRANSLATIONS, IMITATIONS.

SONNETS.

PART I.

A LEGEND OF HARVARD.

THOMAS SARGEANT.

IT was in sixteen seventy-four,
The class went into Latin;
One Thomas Sargeant knew no more
Than Virgil to dead flat in.
Then stern the tutor's forehead grew:
"Disgusted, sir, I am;
How can you such a course pursue?"
Said Thomas Sargeant, "Damn!"

Aghast, the tutor dropped his book:
It fell upon the floor.
The students turned, amazed, to look
On him who'd "swored a swore."
The tutor spoke and said, "Get out!"
And Thomas Sargeant cleared;
His head and heart were tough and stout,
No tutor's wrath he feared.

'T was evening, and the feeble light
  Shone from the Prex's room :
The Faculty, a doleful sight,
  Met in that scene of gloom.
The tutor rose, declared that he
  Was sorry that a lad,
Who might a noble creature be,
  Had uttered words so bad.

They listened all in silence deep,
  Then up stood Doctor Hoar :
He said the College should not sleep,
  When sin was at its door.
"I think," said he, "such things to end,
  That he may not withstand us,
We must T. Sargeant straight suspend,
  Et ipse flagellandus !"

The Faculty approved this course,
  And voted that T. Sargeant
Should be suspended, whipped by force,
  And pay a fine in *argent.*
The President then called, in tones
  Quite the reverse of mealy,

The predecessor of our Jones,
  Whose name was Goodman Hely.

They took Tom to the library;
  They whipped him long and much;
All o'er his body you could see
  Fierce Goodman Hely's touch.
He howled full loudly at the smarts
  Received "before the scholars;"
He went in white and red by starts,
  He came out various colors.

After that day of wrath, no more
  Was Thomas Sargeant seen;
Never again T. Sargeant swore
  Upon the College green.
But often, when on pallet hard,
  Sweet sleep in vain I 'm shamming,
I hear strange noises in the yard,
  And think his ghost is damning.

May 22, 1868.

IN THE TUNNEL.

RIDING up from Bangor,
On the Pullman train,
From a six weeks' shooting
In the woods of Maine;
Quite extensive whiskers,
Beard, moustache as well,
Sat a "student feller,"
Tall and fine and swell.

Empty seat behind him,
No one at his side;
To a pleasant station
Now the train doth glide.
Enter aged couple,
Take the hinder seat;
Enter gentle maiden,
Beautiful, *petite.*

Blushingly she falters,
"Is this seat engaged?"
(See the aged couple
Properly enraged.)
Student, quite ecstatic,
Sees her ticket's "through;"
Thinks of the long tunnel,—
Knows what he will do.

So they sit and chatter,
While the cinders fly,
Till that "student feller"
Gets one in his eye;
And the gentle maiden
Quickly turns about,—
"May I, if you please, sir,
Try to get it out?"

Happy "student feller"
Feels a dainty touch;
Hears a gentle whisper,—
"Does it hurt you much?"
Fizz! ding, dong! a moment
In the tunnel quite,

And a glorious darkness
Black as Egypt's night.

. . . .

Out into the daylight
Darts the Pullman train ;
Student's beaver ruffled
Just the merest grain ;
Maiden's hair is tumbled,
And there soon appeared
Cunning little ear-ring
Caught in student's beard.

November 10, 1871.

"THE OTHER YOUNG MAN."

A CLASS-DAY ROMANCE.

O MOTHER, I 've had a gorgeous time! I
was there from eleven till ten.
Such glorious fun, such a beautiful place, — and,
mother, such splendid men!
Oh, I wish that I were a student! and, mother,
I saw Cousin Ned;
He has grown to be "perfectly lovely," and he
had a still lovelier spread.

For only think, mother, as Fan and I got out
of that horrid car,
Cousin Ned came up with another young man;
so we did n't need dear papa.
But we gave him our shawls and umbrellas to
hold; and Ned, he went off with Fan;
But he introduced me — mother, why do you
frown? — to his comrade, the other young
man.

He was "perfectly splendid!" We went to the
church; and, mother dear, was n't it fun?
I recognized lots of the fellows before the oration
was done.
And, mother dear, what are the "Peelers?" I
thought it a regular sin
For the whole Freshman Class to cry "Peelers!"
and make such a noise coming in.

He carried me round to the spreads, mother, —
it was just like a *matinée* ball;
And then he and I had a *tête-à-tête* in romantic
old Holworthy Hall.
He made me smoke, mother, a wee cigarette; I
drank my first glass of champagne;
And I fibbed when he spilled ice-cream on my
dress, — for I told him it would n't stain.

Then I went to the dance round the Tree,
mother; it was really a beautiful scene, —
Though the Sophomores pushed the poor Fresh-
men around: I thought that was terribly
mean, —

While the Seniors embraced one another with
  such fervent affection and vim,
That, mother, I really felt jealous when I saw
  all his friends hugging *him.*

When he got through that horrible hugging, we
  went to a lot of nice "teas;"
And then we adjourned from the rooms, mother,
  to a quiet spot under the trees.
He was splendid! he said I was lovely. Do
  you think that was quite the right thing?
And, mother, he gave me a keepsake: see, here
  it is, — only a ring.

I spoke to him by his first name, mother; you
  really don't think that he 'd care?
He called me by mine, and *I* did n't. I gave
  him a lock of my hair,
Which he kissed, and then put in his watch,
  mother: and a watch, you know, lies next
  the heart.
Papa cruelly came at the moment, and I, alas!
  had to depart.

He said he would walk to the station: now,
mother dear, was n't that kind?
Ned and Fan made remarks about "spooning,"
and giggled, like children, behind.
But, mother dear, while we were walking — how
nice it was! — down to the car,
He said something "perfectly splendid:" I 'll
tell you to-morrow, mamma.

June 23, 1871.

"THE NOBBY SOPHOMORE."

IT was a nobby Sophomore,
  Was born in Boston town;
Had on his head a little hat,
  On lip a little down;
And nobby trousers, tight as skin,
  On slender legs he wore:
Oh, how the Freshmen longed to be
  The nobby Sophomore!

His coat had broad lappels in front,
  A little tail behind,
Which fluttered as he ran to prayers, —
  A banner on the wind;
Upon his finger shone a ring, —
  A glittering gem it bore:
And who that saw him would not be
  The nobby Sophomore?

A Vandyke collar, long and sharp,
  Without a fold or spot;
A radiant scarf of all the hues,
  Drawn through a golden knot;
Thin ladies-gloves upon his hands,—
  Sixes, perhaps, not more:
A jolly bird! who would not be
  The nobby Sophomore?

The reverend Senior winked at him;
  The Junior looked applause;
The Freshman sighed, "And that is he
  Who makes the College laws!"
And proctors, tutors, professors,
  Passed eyeless by his door:
A jolly life! who would not be
  The nobby Sophomore?

January 15, 1867.

ONLY.

ONLY a small bit of paper,
  With just a few dates, nothing more,
Which at an unfortunate moment
  Glides down from my sleeve to the floor.

Only an Argus-eyed proctor,
  Who, ever upon the *qui vive*,
Picks up with suppressed exultation
  The paper which dropped from my sleeve.

Only four months in the country;
  An extra vacation, that 's all;
But the trade of a proctor still strikes me,
  As something exceedingly small.

February 18, 1876.

AN ANCIENTE BALLADE.

IT was a beauteous mayden,
Moste picturesque to see,
Her architecture was brunette,
Darke as ye sloe was she.
But never having seen a sloe,
We take that backe, for we can't knowe
How darke ye sloe may be.

It also was a studente bolde,
Whose lookes were more than fine
(Though we never meant to call them coarse,
When we beganne that line);
His mien was softe as Dobbs his soape,
His muscles harde as corded rope,
And he played on ye Nine.

It was a rainye nighte in Maye,
When out upon ye streete,
Whome should oure gallant studente, but
This mayden, hap to meet.

She chanced to have no *parapluie*
(Frenche for umbrella); one hadde he,
Whiche warded off ye sleete.

"Faire mayden," then spake he to her,
"Ye storme beats down amain;
Wilt share with me my *parapluie?*
'T will keepe from both ye raine."
'T was smalle, — he feigned that it was large,
Wishing of her to take ye charge;
She to accepte was faine.

Together they meandered onne,
Untille she quoth: "Farewelle!
I 've reached my house." Then he: "Faire mayde,
Thy name, I prithee, telle.
I 'm sure I 've met thee oft before, —
Methinks 't was on ye balle-roome floore:
I knowe thy face fulle welle.

"Thy name shalle be my guiding starre,
Henceforwarde, from this nighte.
I 'll breathe it, inne my orisons,
At breake of morning's lyghte;

At evening, when I seeke repose,
Murmuring thy name, my lippes shalle close,—
'T wille make my dreames more brighte."

Ye mayden looked on him and smiled;
Responsive then beganne:
"My name to you I'd never tell,
In this wide world, young man,
Looked you not so much like my brother.
Listen! your goody is my mother,
My name is Mary Ann!"

November 24, 1871.

HORACE. — ODES : I. 3.

"Among the passengers in the Cunarder on Saturday was President —— of Harvard College."

O POLLUX in the wintry sky,
O pollocks in the frozen seas,
Ye cuttle-fish with baleful eye
(By Verne described), attention, please!
Remorseless sharks with awful tails,
Seals, dolphins, and enormous whales,
E'en each gay automatic porpoise
I pray, be gentle to the corpus
Of him who freights the swift Cunarder.
He is our chief, so don't retard her;
And bear the framer of our laws
In safety to the Cheshire shores,
Unless you wish to draw the tear
From many a hoary Overseer.
Bold was the wretch who dared to stray
First upon ocean's pathless way;
To him, alas! it was no joke,
Although his breast was solid oak,

And brass in triple fold combined
To make his stomach duly lined;
He fell a victim speedily
To scaly Triton's malady,
Giving, as penance for relief,
The major portion of his beef.
Such is each mortal's hapless plight
Who seeks the realms of Amphitrite.
Columbus, when he saw that speck
Of land, was pallid on the deck;
E'en that renowned sea-dog, De Soto,
Went inside out at first *in toto.*
While Palinurus, sadly floored,
Followed his dinner overboard;
And Noah ate first, unless books lie,
The doves he afterwards let fly.
So, Neptune, grant our master dear
Refreshing draughts of ginger beer,
A downy bed, with pillows soft
(A lower berth, not one aloft,
Which does not slope too much to leeward),
A kindly ceremonious steward;
And bid your crew to gently shake
Our chief for Alma Mater's sake.

But he who ocean tries must hope
With horrors numberless to cope.
There frown the icebergs cold and gross,
Or "banks" far worse than "scopulos;"
While even "tristes Hyadas"
Are lesser ill than loss of gas;
While "Aquilo" is nothing to
The motion of that awful screw.
But why did Heaven separate
By boundless ocean state from state,
If mortals rash infringe her laws
With steamships, rams, and monitors?
Or ruthless send a cable through
The croquet ground the Nereids drew,
And fright those dears that ocean pickles
With frequent telegrams to Sickles?
But man is naughty, bad, and runs
Through wickedness as babes through buns.
Nought to the human mind is hard,
Unless it be the College Yard
(Now that the plank walks are laid down).
Our actions cause old Jove to frown.
The heavens themselves, 't is whispered, soon
Jules Verne will seek (he 's tried the moon);

And Jove, though loth to interfere,
Will make him walk off on his ear.
Oh, why won't men let up such stuff?
Jove has sent thunderbolts enough!

February 6, 1874.

MEMENTOS.

LOQUITUR M. A., *searching in writing-desk for a crimson tie on the morning of June* 25, 1875.]

A LITTLE, crumpled, dainty glove!
Pearl-colored once, now mottled:
The cause, a most unlucky shove
Of champagne badly bottled.
'T was very small, — I mean Maud's hand;
How it returned my pressure,
As I said, "That 's you!" when the band
Was playing "Little Treasure!"
I stole it from her in the Square,
While waiting for the carriage;
Last week I read, and did n't care,
The notice of her marriage.
Although I really think she might
Have sent an invitation,
In memory of that Class-Day night
And our half-hour's flirtation.

. . . .

That crimson ribbon, — let me see!
  Yes, that belonged to Florence:
She was as jolly as could be,
  Although it rained in torrents.
I met her at her brother's spread;
  How she loved water-ices!
He had the Prex there, and she said
  Had also all the *Vices!*
She wished to dance, and so we walked
  Across to Massachusetts;
I pushed, she tore her dress, we talked
  And danced, I think, in two sets.
The ribbon dropped, — 't was very queer! —
  Unfastened from her shoulder: —
She has grown homely, so I hear;
  And I, — well, I 've grown older.

. . . . . .

A little bunch of faded flowers,
  Pinks, heliotrope, and roses;
Obituary of the hours
  When they — and I — were Josie's.
She was the nicest of them all,
  But would talk slang to *mater;*

I know she cut me at the ball,
  And almost made me hate her.
That Class Day was almost as hot
  As this one will by noon be: —
"*Is papa ready?*" Precious Tot!
  Tell mamma that he 'll soon be.
Flowers, ribbon, glove, go back again!
  Three days of pleasure summing:
The mem'ries that you bring give pain: —
"*I hear you, Grace! I'm coming!*"

June 25, 1875.

THE OLD PROFESSOR.

THE old professor taught no more,
  But lingered round the college walks ;—
Stories of him we boys told o'er,
  Before the fire, in evening talks.
I 'll ne'er forget how he came in
  To recitation, one March night,
And asked our tutor to begin,
" And let me hear these boys recite."

As we passed out, we heard him say,
" Pray leave me here a while, alone.
Here in my old place let me stay
  Just as I did in years long flown."
Our tutor smiled and bowed consent,
  Rose courteous from his high-backed chair,
And down the darkening stairs he went,
  Leaving the old professor there.

The lecture room was dark and bare,
  The old professor sat alone:
The bust of Virgil seemed to stare
  Upon him with its eyes of stone.
The lights shone here and there, outside;
  The last class down the stairs had rushed;
Stillness spread through the entries wide,
  In every room all noise was hushed.

From out the shadows faces seemed
  To look on him in his old place, —
Fresh faces that with radiance beamed,
  Radiance of boyish hope and grace;
And faces that had lost their youth,
  Although in years they still were young;
And faces o'er whose love and truth
  The funeral anthem had been sung.

"These are my boys," he murmured then,
  "My boys, as in the years long past;
Though some are angels, others men,
  Still as my boys I hold them fast.
There 's one don 't know his lesson now,
  That one of me is making fun,

And that one 's cheating: — ah! I see,
I see and love them every one.

"And is it then so long ago
This chapter in my life was told,
Did all of them thus come and go,
And have I really grown so old?
No! here are my old pains and joys,
My book once more is in my hand,
Once more I hear these very boys,
And seek their hearts to understand."

. . . .

They found him there with open book,
And eyes closed with a calm content;
The same old sweetness in his look
There used to be when fellows went
To ask him questions and to talk,
When recitations were all o'er; —
We saw him in the college walk
And in his former place no more.

December 10, 1869.

GRINDING.

"Vagrants whose arts
Have caged some devil in their mad machine."
— *O. W. Holmes.*

'TWAS near the Semi-annuals,
  The Saturday before;
Distinctly memory recalls
  Those blessed hours of yore.
The sunbeams seemed, that afternoon,
  To their own warmth to draw
The earth, until it seemed like June, —
  That February thaw.

My heart I curbed for study's sake;
  I left the world behind,
And solemnly resolved to take
  An everlasting grind.
My grate was filled with Freshman coke
  (My coal was somewhat low),
When I began to sport my oak,
  And interview *Ganot.*

My love for Physics had, I fear,
  Been all too slight before;
I counted it throughout the year
  An illustrated bore.
And when conditions, night by night,
  Came in my dreams to me,
I wished *Ganot* was out of sight,
  And buried in the sea.

The street was full of sounds erelong,
  My solitude to mar;
The discord changed into a song, —
"It was my last cigar."
My windows straight were shut in vain:
  Too well, alas! I knew
It was the organ-grinder's strain, —
  And he was grinding, too.

Then, being suffered to commence,
  Through all his list he ran,
To gratify his audience,
  And yet again began,
Repeating those which all prefer, —
"My darling, dearest May;"

And, what I really wished he were, —
  "Ten thousand miles away."

For Physics I was all unmanned.
  And is there one who thinks
That he could study with a band
  Performing "Captain Jinks?"
I showered my pence in hopes, of course,
  He would the sooner cease.
For says *Ganot:* "Increase the force;
  The time will then decrease."

At last the sound a moment ceased;
  I hoped, but hoped in vain,
That he had crossed Main Street at least,
  If not the "raging main."
A moment only: it was o'er, —
  A respite brief as sweet, —
And then he played them all once more,
  Though no one cried, "Repeat."

A dirge played through the honeymoon,
  A whistled round at grace,
"Old Hundred" for a dancing tune,
  Are something out of place.

Nor is the fitness more, I ween,
  When through the silent halls
Is heard the grinder's "mad machine"
  At Semi-annuals.

And this alone I learned from all
  My weary, misspent hours,
To wit: that powers mechanical
  Are unlike mental powers.
My mind I found, with late remorse,
  The more and more I tried,
Gave constantly decreasing force
  Tangentially applied.

February 6, 1874.

THE LAY OF THE BELL.

FOR many years, in this high place,
'Mid wind and rain I 've hung,
And gained renown for eloquence
By holding fast my tongue.
But now my yoke of servitude
Is growing hard to wear;
Although my yoke, I doubt not, has
A greater weight to bear.

I serve a very cruel man,
Who rings me from below;
From him I cannot wring a tear
Of pity for my woe.
He comes to me when first he wakes
And turns me upside down.
Then swings me round, so very hard
I fear he 'll crack my crown.

Although 't is hard to suffer so,
  I like to see my power;
For all the world comes trooping forth,
  When I proclaim the hour.
When first I ring at early morn,
  'T is true that no one cares;
But when I call the second time,
  They all rush out to prayers.

O ye who, when the weather 's cold,
  Can hardly see the fun
Of getting up, while still 't is dark,
  To take a little run,
Pray pity my hard lot, and think
  How very cold you 'd feel
If 'stead of dressing when you rose,
  You had to rise and peal.

My duty is to tell the hour;
  And, though I 'm brassy bold,
I never dare to speak aloud
  Unless I first am tolled.
Each hour I call the trembling souls
  To what they so much dread,

And mournfully bewail the fate
  Of those already dead.

I 've heard that wicked men sometimes
  Were broken on the wheel;
And, though I am not broken yet,
  I know just how they feel.
I cannot see what I have done
  That they have tied me fast;
So, patiently, I 'll wait the time
  When I shall ring my last.

November 25, 1867.

ELECTIVES.

COME hither, gentle Freshman,
And recline beside my chair,
While I for coming duties
Your untutored mind prepare.
In this enterprising College,
As you 're not too young to know,
The grand elective system
Is at present " all the go."

And in his education
Every man can have a voice;
And, when he 's paid his money,
He 's allowed to take his choice.
The time will come when you must choose
What courses you 'll pursue,
And my experience may prove
Of benefit to you.

While yet a Freshman, you will be
  Presented by the College
With a pamphlet, pointing out to you
  The different sorts of knowledge.
The great conundrum then becomes:
  Where are you going to find
The maximum of learning,
  With the minimum of grind?

There are courses in the classics,
  In the languages defunct,
Where the busy bees make rushes,
  And the drones are rudely flunked.
In the gay and festive Sanskrit
  You 'd a cheerful pastime find;
And, investigating Hebrew,
  You might leave dull care behind.

If you fancy mathematics,
  You can suit yourself with ease, —
As for me, it turns my stomach,
  And it makes my vitals freeze,
To think of sines and tangents,
  Algebra or Calculus;

And I pray, "From all such misery,
 Good Lord, deliver us!"

But if you have æsthetic tastes,
 And wish to hold your own
In the glorious *bas bleu* circles
 Of New England's greatest town, —
You must take a course in Fine Arts,
 And learn to tell at sight
A chromo from a crayon sketch,
 And be positive you 're right.

But where'er your tastes may lead you,
 And whate'er may be your choice,
Attend to this I tell you,
 And heed well my warning voice:
Never elect a study which
 Is "mighty soft," you 're told;
For, ten to one, you 'll find yourself
 Most miserably sold.

Now, to quote a bit of Scripture,
 Which I 'm sure is *apropos*,

A camel through the needle's eye
  More easily can go,
Than a gentleman of leisure,
  With a mind unused to toil,
Can get through on his electives,
  And not burn the midnight oil.

November 5, 1875.

THE TABULAR VIEW.

WITH shirt-collar rumpled and torn, by a
feeble flickering light,
With despondent look and gestures too awful
for human sight,
With eyes of a maniac lustre, and cheeks of a
livid hue,
A gentleman sat at his table composing the
"Tabular View."

With his head in a cold-water bandage, he
worked there two months and a half;
No cares could distract his attention, no diver-
sion could draw forth a laugh;
He sat there a slave to stern duty, till one
night at a quarter past two
He glanced at the clock, — shuddered, — fainted:
he had finished the "Tabular View."

All scornful the printer received it, exclaiming
"It 's all very nice,
But doubtless you know the old proverb that 'a
cat never burns her paws twice!'
I ain't been a-printing these ten years without
learning an odd thing or two,
And I 've had, my dear sir, the misfortune to
print *once* the 'Tabular View!'"

The gentleman paused for a moment, then drew
forth a purse full of gold;
That printer was poor, and he knew it, that
printer was white-haired and old;
And his name, — but I guess I won't tell it, it
can't be of interest to you,
For he 's now in an insane asylum: — he printed
the "Tabular View."

They were finished and duly delivered through
the College from Hollis to Thayer,
And the gentleman sat in his office with a mind
free from trouble and care.
A knock at the door: — and a Freshman! — all
livid that gentleman grew,

When the Freshman exclaimed, "I have found,
sir, a mistake in the 'Tabular View!'"

That gentleman leaped from his arm-chair; there
burst through the wide-open door
A Sophomore, Junior, and Senior; — of Fresh-
men a dozen or more.
"O sir," said the Sophomore wildly, "my head's
in a deuce of a stew, —
I have for this hour six studies set down in the
'Tabular View.'"

. . . . . .

'T was night and the students were sleeping,
't was midnight and bitterly cold,
As through the broad gate of Mount Auburn
a hearse and three carriages rolled: —
A rattle of spades in the darkness; a sob and
a whisper or two —
There's a bill to be paid at Pike's stable; —
this comes of the "Tabular View!"

March 10, 1871.

A MIDNIGHT SOLILOQUY.

[SCENE: *A room in Matthews.* HOUR: *eleven o'clock. Student, retiring, soliloquizes.*]

HEGEL, and Kant, and Fichte, and Descartes,
Now fill my poor head with I scarce know what.
Subjective truths and formal principles,
Sufficient reason's awful fourfold root,
Antinomies of reason and paralogisms
Whirl in my head, that almost bursts with isms.
Shades of the Ego that transcendeth sense,
And of ideals that never may be real,
Haunt not my sleeping as my waking hours!
Leave me in peace until the fatal day!

[*Opens the window and retires.*]

What quiet reigns in Alma Mater's groves!
How cool the night breeze plays upon my brow,
Bearing no sound to break the sweet repose,
Save the green branches' rustling lullaby!

[*Dog in Grays howls dismally.*]

Grant that the news be true, I lately heard,
That these vile curs that desecrate the night,
And murder sleep, have met at last the eye
Of that lame Nemesis, the Faculty,
And shortly will be exiled from the Yard.

[*Students enter the yard, singing, "Carry me back" vociferously, and disperse with howls.*]

What sympathy and anger moved us all
When brutul "peelers" set upon those men,
Who made the night melodious with French airs,
And dragged them manacled to dungeons deep!
But now, if one ill word I uttered then
Has pierced one conscientious "peeler's" heart,
I humbly beg forgiveness for the deed.
And when we heard of that chief justice bold
Who once a rash policeman met at night,
And dared to speak in operatic strains, —
The triumph of that justice was our own.
Of that policeman, too, I ask forgiveness.
Would that a watchful guardian of the night
Behind each tree took up his nightly stand,
Armed well with gyves, and clubs, and "twisters" strong,

Then wrong would be averted, or else justice
served.
But now 't is still again, I 'll seize the time
To take in sleep a refuge from my cares.

[*Man by Weld shouts to man near Matthews:* "*Bill!*" (*Silence.*) "BILL!" (*No answer.*) "BILL!" *Matthews man:* "*What?*" *Weld man:* "*Got a cigarette paper?*" *Matthews:* "*No.*" *Weld:* "*All right.*" *Short silence, followed by* "*Thousand and One Nights,*" *played on the piano in the next room.*]

O cruel fate, that damns me to lie still,
And bear this wanton theft of needful rest!
Is this fair Harvard's influence of good?
Are these her sons fed on elective food?
Perhaps these roysterers have read for hours
The ethics wise of Calderwood or Kant,
Yet who among them cares to shape his acts
By maxims that conform to moral law?
Oh! give me but one bowl of water hot,
And but one gathering 'neath my window ledge.
Give me but this! I pray, I ask no more.

[*Tosses restlessly upon his pillow. A clattering is heard on the stairs, as of some one ascending them with difficulty. The* "*Miserere*" *from* "*Trovatore*" *is then heard, sung very loud and very drunkenly. Student sits bolt upright.*]

Death and destruction seize upon the wretch
Whose evil cat-calls strike no proctor's ear.
How hard it is to lie thus impotent!
A pillow serves to slay mosquitoes shrill,
A boot, perchance, the nightly rat may still,
But 'gainst this outrage vile my wrath is vain,
And grows by feeding on itself, until
For lack of vent it makes me almost mad.

[*Attacks the bolster fiercely.*]

Alas! my brain is whirling, and my nerves,
Now all unstrung, resist th' approach of sleep.

[*Falls into an uncertain doze. Several particularly large cannon crackers go off on the esplanade, and a rocket aimed from across the yard enters the window and strikes the wall about a foot from the student's head. Shrieks from the various buildings are heard without. Sparks, golden rain, and silver stars illuminate the room, while the rocket hisses out its life upon the floor. Student leaps up.*]

Where am I? — Oh, what hellish visitor —
These shrieks, these loud reports that rend the
air, —

What fiend has come to claim me for his prey?
My limbs refuse to bear me! Oh, my head!
All that I see in one blank whirl is lost,
And all I hear is merged in one vague roar.

[*Swoons, and curtain falls.*]

June 25, 1875.

NEMESIS.

SCENE, a crowded horse-car:
  Enter youthful dame;
Gallant student rises,
  Tutor does the same.
Smiles she on the former,
  With a glance so sweet,
That his heart throbs wildly
  As she takes *his* seat.

Tutor, in the corner,
  Sits and bites his thumb;
Student smiles to see him
  Sulking, overcome.
Maiden sits demurely,
  Drops a dainty glove:
Such a chance the student
  Hastens to improve.

Maiden wants a window
  Just behind her lowered:
Beckons she the student.
  Tutor is ignored.
As the window closes,
  With a sudden slam,
Tutor mutters something
  Very like a — hem.

Then a conversation,
  Soft and low, ensues:
Student asks a favor,
  Maiden don't refuse;
Fastens pink securely
  In his button-hole.
Tutor calls, not blessings,
  Down on student's soul.

Now all ye who envy
  Much our student's fate,
Know the dreadful sequel, —
  Learn how tutors hate;

Know the direful vengeance
  Of a tutor scorned :
Next examination,
  Gallant student warned.

April 27, 1872.

"ONLY ONCE AGAIN."

ONCE, upon a midnight dreary, when of cards I had grown weary,
And the bottle, with the tumblers, lay quite emptied on the floor;
As I sat at ease reclining, by the firelight faintly shining,
Suddenly I heard a whining, through the key-hole of my door.
Bolt upright I quickly started, and I leaped upon the floor,
While I barely muttered, "Pshaw!"

How the sharp, spasmodic clicking, which the clock then made while ticking,
Made me shake and quake with terror, as I never had before;
So that now to stop the swaying of my system I stood saying,

"'T is some 'bummah' who 's been staying, dissipating, at some store,—
Some poor 'bummah' who 's mistaken just the number of his door.
This it is, and nothing more."

Then I flung the door asunder, and I gazed, in speechless wonder,
As I saw a figure enter, hopping through the opened door.
Like an elf he was in fable, and arrayed in blackest sable;
Skipped upon my study-table, just three feet from off the floor,—
And he sat there, grinned and chuckled, just three feet from off the floor.
In his hand a scroll he bore.

Then this curious imp dispelling all the thoughts I had for yelling,
By his cheerful grin so luring, and the parchment that he bore,—
I gazed on as it extended, till I saw my own name blended

With some more to be "suspended," if I "cut" but one prayer more,
And we all should be "suspended," if we "cut" but one prayer more.
I had "cut" just ninety-four.

"Imp," I cried, "thou puny creature, knavish in thy every feature,
By whate'er is sacred to thee, tell me now, I do implore,
If by punctual attendance, and sincere, contrite repentance,
I may yet escape this sentence, by not cutting one prayer more?
Yet escape this awful sentence by not cutting one prayer more."
Then the imp said, "Nevermore."

"Wretched imp!" I fiercely shouted, "be that word forever doubted.
Leave my room, and leave my presence; leave," I cried, "for evermore!
Take thy form of blackest sable quickly from my study-table;

Leave," I shrieked, "while yet you're able!"
and I hurled him from the door;
And I seized him by the collar, and I kicked
him from the door.
And he vanished through the floor.

But his figure ever haunts me, and that word
forever taunts me,
For each day it deeper, deeper, sinks into my
bosom's core;
And each morning finds me springing, at the
prayer-bell's early ringing,
And, before it ceases dinging, I have reached
the Chapel door;
And my soul, inspired by music which it finds
within that door,
Aims to "cut"—ah!—nevermore.

April 12, 1872.

VACATION.

HAPPY thoughts of happy days
Passed in pleasant places;
Blindly walking crooked ways
Led by pretty faces.

Dreams of dances, smiles, and sighs,
Now and then a quarrel ;
Stories read in lowered eyes,
Each with fitting moral.

Odd gloves, scraps of ribbon, tell
Tales of mild flirtation ;
Faded flowers — There goes the bell !
I 'm late for recitation.

October 14, 1869.

THE GIRL IN BLUE.

OH, have you seen the girl in blue
  Who lives far down the avenue?
    With modest eye
    She passeth by,—
The girl on the avenue.

Her jaunty bonnet, frail and small—
A ribbon and a rose are all;—
    But hair of gold,
    Beneath it rolled,
Crowns the girl on the avenue.

Her rolling collar gives to sight
A tender throat and lily-white;
    And gems and rings
    And nameless things
Wears the girl on the avenue.

A sweet, soft hand for mine to grasp:
A slender waist for me to clasp;
    Your little foot!
    Its dainty boot!
Dear girl on the avenue!

O lips as red as roses are!
O eyes as bright as gem or star!
    To gaze is bliss;
    What were to kiss?
Sweet girl on the avenue!

Your cheek's fresh rose should never fade,
Fair head, here! on my shoulder laid!
    The hours run fleet,
    But life is sweet;
Ah, girl on the avenue.

November 1, 1867.

PROGRAMME FOR THE RECEPTION OF G. D. ALEXIS, SON OF THE CZAR.

THE whole Senior class in a body, in swallow-tailed coats and white ties,
Will assemble to welcome the G. D., at a few minutes after sunrise,
In front of the horse railroad station, which will be fitted up very nice,
The company having consented to bring the Duke out at half price.

It is said that Alexis will donate a couple of tame Russian bears
To the College the moment he gets here ; he will then be conducted to " prayers."
The G. D. will read the whole service, if he can, in his own mother-tongue,
And after his praying is over the great Russian hymn will be sung.

Alexis will breakfast at Commons. The students are begged not to shout;
And also to eat very little, as the spring chickens may not hold out.
From breakfast he 'll go to Gymnasium, — after seeing some Sophomores haze, —
Where he 'll put up "the hundred-pound dumb-bell," and perform on the "flying trapeze."

After viewing Memorial Building and the lions of our Institution,
He will then hear the Juniors in Spanish, the Freshmen recite elocution;
Subscribe to the "Advocate," boat club, base ball club, and all the societies;
Shake hands with the Goodies, the chief of police, and other such great notorieties.

The Faculty will hold a meeting, to let our great visitor see
Our fine educational system. He will then be elected A. B.,
And possibly tutor in Russian. And I should n't wonder at all

If he gave in return a few millions to found an
Alexian Hall.

The "Tragedy" will be repeated, by express permit of the Dean;
A chance will be given Alexis to see the "infernal machine."
The chief of police will be blown into infinite fragments no doubt;
The "Sophs" put in bonds for ten thousand,—Alexis will bail them all out.

To please the Grand Duke, in the evening, Weld Hall will be burned to the ground,
With all the available lumber belonging to neighbors around;
The Glee Club will sing all the evening; the fire department will swear,
While proctors will flock in large numbers, for the purpose of—taking the air.

As he goes to the ball in the evening, his visit will thus be cut short;

The whole Freshman class will attend him in triumph as far as the 'Port.
The company kindly have offered an exquisite new special car.
We trust the "draw" will not detain him. Long life to the son of the Czar!

December 8, 1871.

"WHAT IS THAT, MOTHER?"

"WHAT is that mother?"
"The Freshman, child:
Just from his home, gentle, humble, and mild.
Quick as the sound of the bell strikes his ears,
He 's up and away, ere his tutor appears.
He knows what 's a *fizzle*, and, worse, what 's a *dead;*
But best, how to *squirt* proofs, *out of his head.*
Ever, my child, let thy life's young days
Appear, like the Freshman, deserving of praise."

"What is that, mother?"
"The Soph, my son:
Is n't he glad that his first year is done!
See him espying his prey from afar, —
'Holloa there, you Freshman, let 's have a cigar!'
He lights it, and walks through the street like a god:

To his classmates, a smile; to the 'Fresh,' *just*
a nod.
My son, try to copy the Sophomore in this:
Pass a year of your life in perpetual bliss."

"What is that, mother?"
"The Junior, boy:
Proudly completing his course with joy.
He thinks of the Freshman as quite in the way;
The jokes of the Sophomores are silly, *passé*.
He talks of *professions*, and what he will be,
When from college and lessons he 's perfectly
free.
My boy, let this trait of the Junior be thine:
Have a look on your face of the deepest de-
sign."

"What is that, mother?"
"The Senior, sweet:
He is sailing onward, the world to meet.
He 'll soon have no masters, must act for him-
self,
And engage in the strife for the ignoble pelf.
And he turns, on his Class Day, a last look to
seek,

With a tear in his eye which, God knows, is n't
weak.

My child, when you turn from a loved place to
leave,

May you, like the Senior, kind wishes receive."

April 12, 1872.

THE CRIMSON AND THE BLUE.

AN INCIDENT OF THE WORCESTER REGATTA.

HER brother was a man of Yale,
 A member of the crew;
And so she came the race to see,
 Festooned with bows of blue,
When a horrid crimson Harvard boy
 Stood just within her view.

They started — and the crowd was wild;
 She felt herself grow pale:
Still, as that boy yelled "Harvard" forth,
 She sang out, "Yale! Yale!! Yale!!!"
And the boats shot past, and no one knew
 Which would at last prevail.

"Oh, which is leading now?" she cried,
 Unmindful of the showers
Which poured upon her gauzy robes,
 And her little hat's blue flowers;

Then that Harvard boy turned round and said,
"I 'm afraid that it is ours."

It was so very gracefully
And delicately said,
That beneath her eyes of true Yale blue,
Her cheeks flushed Harvard red;
And all of her antipathy
For that Harvard boy had fled.

That evening her big brother said,
"It still has been of use,
Our coming here, although I own
The Harvards cooked our goose;
Since I have met a Harvard friend
Whom I must introduce."

And so he did. Again the red
Rushed over her sweet face,
Again she thought that Harvard boy
Showed gentlemanly grace;
And in spite of her spoiled dress, declared
Worcester a charming place.

. . . . . .

I know two lovers; but their names
  To tell I do refuse;
A new engagement is announced,
  But I will not say whose,
But will simply offer as a toast,
  "The Crimsons and the Blues!"

December 24, 1869.

SOME POETICAL MOLECULES.

SOME time ago the Editors of the "Advocate," finding that the poetical effusions published in that journal were greeted — to use a mild expression — with anathemas, resolved that, for the encouragement of their poetical corps, they would address the following circular to the leading poets of England and America: —

"SIR, — The "Harvard Advocate" will be perfectly willing to publish, free of charge, any of the poetical efforts of your youthful days. It consents to do this for the sake of encouraging the youthful poets of this University.

"Very respectfully,

"THE EDITORS OF THE 'ADVOCATE.'"

After petitioning the Faculty for permission to send this circular away, copies of it were dispatched to the most eminent of living poets. The fame of the "Advocate" made most bards very eager to write for it, and many answers containing contributions were received. Feeling that some recompense ought to be given to these distinguished men, the Editors determined to award, as a prize for the best poem, a magnificent sewing-machine, to be paid for from the proceeds of bills then due the paper. Two things have prevented the execution of this noble intention: first, no contribution was good enough; and, secondly, those bills have not yet been paid.

We select from the enormous number of articles sent us the following ode from the rising light of American literature: —

TO A SWILL-CART.

BY W—LT WH—TM—N.

INCOMPREHENSIBLE swill-cart!
Are you aware that you fill me with wonder?
What things have been in you!
What things may yet be in you!
Does n't your owner (probably a Hibernian) often tire of you as a means of obtaining his daily meals, the chief ingredient in which is the wholesome potato?
Swill-cart, you are like life, and men are like swill.
Pah!
Likewise "Ugh!"
You make me sick, O swill-cart! and I drive you from my mind.

We have received from one of Harvard's most distinguished sons several poems to be read at the annual reunions of his old class, in 1869, 1870, 1871, 1872, and so on. He requests us to use but one, as the others are intended for the columns of the "Atlantic Monthly." As no one of these poems is less than thirty stanzas in length, we publish three stanzas of his poem for next year: —

THE JOLLY OLD BOYS.

BY O. W. H–LM–S, M. D.

1829 — 1869.

TOGETHER we 've met for a jolly old row;
Let the life-blood flow fast through our arteries and veins,
And when comes to-morrow, let no one know how
This table-cloth met with so many red stains.

. . . . . .

Here is Smith, who is fat, and Brown, who 's all bones,
And, as I read on, it excites them to glee;
While cerebral movements still agitate Jones;
And my shyness prevents me from speaking of me.

. . . . . .

Dear boys, when we die and in Heaven we stand,
And our hearts are delighted with happier joys,
The angels will ask, "Who are those, hand in hand?"
And this will we answer, "Lord, we are 'the Boys.'"

Should space permit us at some future time, we will give the contributions of Wh–tt–r, L–w–ll, Sw–nb–rne, Br–wn–ng, and very many others who have attempted to achieve immortality by sending their productions to the "Advocate."

April 23, 1868.

. . . .

In accordance with many requests, and with a partial promise made a year ago, we lay before our readers the second and last instalment of our contributions from distinguished poets. Without further preliminary, then, we begin with

RED HOT.

BY A. C. SW–NB–RNE.

HER purple cheeks are hot with wine,
She sits crowned with a clustering vine,
And dripping is her hair;

All glowing are her humid lips,
And scorching are her finger tips;
She is divinely fair.

She panteth with the summer heat;
The heavy air is warm and sweet,
Like incense on a fire.
With languor all her form is rife.
What is the greatest joy of life?
To love and to perspire.

In beautiful contrast with these glowing lines are the following verses: —

SONG OF THE MUCKERS.

BY WM. M—RR—S.

O STUDENTS! see, we stand here in the Yard;
The grass is turf, and like our lives is hard:
Oh, scramble cents, and we will go away.

"Depart, depart, we have no cents to-day."

If we run home, our weary way is drear;
Certes, by water wan and fir-trees sere;
Yet scramble cents, and we will go away.

"Depart, depart, we have no cents to-day."

We will depart and leave you in sweet peace;
O'er the brown hills our echoing song shall
cease,
If you will only scramble cents to-day.

"Well, here are cents, if you will go away."

The tortures of the damned run through each
vein,
These cents are fiery hot and full of pain;
O students! now indeed we go away.

"Farewell, farewell, and come no other day."

We have reserved, for our last and choicest, a short contribution by the great dramatic poet. Many others have written, but the "Advocate" is a student's paper, and we shall never after this give encouragement to any outside poets, however distinguished:—

OBTRUSIONS IN ÆVO.

BY R–B–RT BR–WN–NG.

[*He speaks.*]

I' THE past, well what i' the past, — fancies, perhaps;
Is it not so, my Lippi? Very well,
Suppose the artist so to counterfeit,
Until you see the rugged visage glower,
Full of dead, reeking venom, foul stuff, boy.
But this is brain work. True for you again.
Gratias agimus, and I might add, *tibi;*
But then I hate — pshaw — sing to us, my girl.

[*She sings.*]

One, two, three,
What do you see
To make you think she will faithful be?
Were she a man,
The Tartar khan
Would return to where he began.

[*He thinks.*]

A life skims off its lees, and there you are.
Suppose it clarified; we ask, what then?
Nothing save that this burrowing mole i' the
earth, —
But 't is the wine. Oh! no, 't is but the truth!
And Lippi knows — hey, Bentivoglio?
Murder must come, while golden is the ring,
Murder must come, thou seest it, dear Lord.
Away with all misgivings. Come, — to bed!

May 14, 1869.

AN IDYL OF THE KING.

AND now was Christmas-tide at Camelot;
And Arthur's heart was joyful, seeing then
How all was gleesome at the Table Round.
But Guinevere was sad, for much she feared
That, when the King sat at his meat that day,
The kitchen knaves would cause for her great shame.
A wondrous dish, in sooth, she had prepared,—
A score of warblers from the forest green,
And four besides, all baked in one great pie,—
A meet repast for Arthur and his knights.
But well the Queen knew cunning Merlin's skill,
And how that Vivian had beguiled the man,
And hated her, the spotless Arthur's spouse,
Because she would herself have him to lord.
So then the Queen sat fearful at the board,
And Arthur took the carving-knife in hand,
And sweetly spake he to Queen Guinevere,—
"My dear, will you take pork, or blackbird pie?"

And she, to still defer what most she feared,
Said "Pork," and Arthur sent her roasted swine.
Then turned to Launcelot, bravest and best loved
Of all the knights about the Table Round,
And said to him, "Old boy, what will you have?"
And Launcelot said, "I 'll take some blackbird
 pie."
Then came a smile o'er wily Vivian's face;
But Merlin sage looked grave, yet chuckled low,
While Arthur with his knife pried up the crust.
And when the pie was opened, then the birds
'Gan all to sing; and Guinevere turned red,
Then pale, and fainted, for she knew full well
How all the ladies fair in Arthur's court
Would say she was no housewife, and that they
Could not see how the King put up with her.
But Launcelot consoled her. "Guinevere,
Cheer up!" he said; "since well you know the
 King
Had parents none, and so will never say,
'My mother could have made a better pie.'"

January 19, 1874.

THE OLD INNKEEPER.

BEYOND the little village church,
  Where the road turns off below,
The old inn stood, just by the wood,
  A long, long time ago.
The host he was a merry man,
  Hearty and stout and hale;
And, with a laugh, he used to quaff
  His good wife's home-brewed ale.
"For some," said he, "must wealthy be,
  Some high-born and some low;
But all men can have jollity,
  Wherever they may go."

If e'er his wife did scold at him
  Because he drank full oft,
And cried out "Shame," with words of blame,
  He 'd mix a larger draught.
He sent no beggar from his door;
  Did poor man ever come

To pass that way, he 'd make him stay;
His inn was like a home.
"For some," said he, "must wealthy be,
But here 's a man so low
That all should give him jollity,
Wherever he may go."

In winter, when the roads around
Were covered with the snow,
His cheerful light gleamed on the sight,
And there all men would go.
With pipes and glasses in their hands,
Before a blazing fire,
With jest and song, time passed along,
Nor could one ever tire.
"For all," said he, "can merry be,
Whether they 're high or low;
Here 's health to mirth and jollity,
And may they with us go!"

Though Time drew furrows o'er his brow,
It never caused a sigh,
Since every year with hearty cheer
So merrily flew by.

And when his sickness came, and all
  Declared that he must die,
On his death-bed he only said
  To his wife, Margery,
"Remember me, when dead I be,
  For, though I leave you so,
I shall have mirth and jollity,
  Wherever I may go."

They carried him unto his grave;
  The sun shone warm and bright;
The burial-ground, for far around,
  Was bathed in golden light.
Said one grave-digger to his mate,
  "Although I do not know
Where is to be his future state,
  Above us or below,
This thing," said he, "is clear to me,
  He loved enjoyment so,
He 'll pass his days in jollity,
  Wherever he may go."

November 9, 1866.

THE SENIOR.

"AH! I was a Freshman then,
And 't was very long ago."

In a voice both low and tender,
With his feet upon the fender,
From the clouds around his head,
This is what the Senior said.

He was tall and very thin,
But graceful, like some ancient column;
Wan and sallow was his skin,
And his voice both deep and solemn.
Lazily he leaned him there,
By the roaring fire's glare,
In a wondrous easy-chair,
Head aback, and knees in air.
In his hand, with greatest care,

As of sudden danger fearsome, —
Bowl so brown and rich and rare,
Held he forth a mighty meerschaum;
Day and night, and day again,
Smoked in joy, and smoked in pain,
It had got that precious stain.
By the side of the Senior tall,
On a table neat and small,
Gleaming richly, did appear
Two glasses and a pot of beer.

Some remark that I had uttered,
As the fire roared and sputtered,
Seemed to touch him to the core.
For my bended eyes were caught
By his slippers, strangely wrought;
So I asked just this, — no more, —
Who had wove the rare design,
Where the clustered roses twine,
Deftly worked in green and gold,
On the slippers worn and old.

In a voice both low and tender,
With his feet upon the fender,

This is what the Senior said:
"Ah! I was a Freshman then,
And 't was very long ago."

Silently he puffed awhile,
Till from the clouds there broke a smile.
Then he told with animation,
How he met her, one vacation,
In a farm-house by the ocean;
Pictured then, with deep emotion,
All the beauty of the fair;
Golden lustre of her hair;
Beaming eyes of tender blue,
Dainty lashes peeping through;
And a simple way she had
Of looking sometimes sweetly sad, —
But I will not tell you more
Of a story told before:
How they had a lover's quarrel;
Nor expatiate on the moral,
The bitter moral that he drew;
Not even this will tell to you.

When, at last, 't was very late,
"Stay!" he said, "a moment wait!"
As I left him, bowing low.
Then he filled the glasses high,
With half a laugh and half a sigh:
"We 'll drink the maid of long ago!"
Then, as there I stopped to linger,
As the dying fire-light shone,
I marked a ring upon his finger,
With initials not his own.

Yet in voice both low and tender,
With his feet upon the fender,
From the clouds around his head,
This is what the Senior said:
"Ah! I was a Freshman then,
And 't was very long ago."

January 19, 1871.

MILTON'S ANSWER.

ONE day, Lord Roxburgh, of high repute,
In mien agreeable, in address, acute,
Praised Milton's wife before him (you 'll excuse
My calling her the shrewest of all shrews).

He drew a little simile in prose,
And said, "She was as fair as any rose."
List to the answer: it was very wise,
One of the sagest of all sage replies.

"Your lordship knows the blindness of my sight
Forbids my being judge of flowers bright;
But yet you speak the truth, not praise or scorn
For of that rose I feel a daily thorn."

April 2, 1875.

POPPING THE QUESTION.

I KNEW by his looks what he 'd come for: I
plainly had seen from the first
It must come to this sooner or later, and I 'd
made up my mind for the worst.
So I hid myself under the curtains, where the
loving pair could n't see me,
In order to watch their proceedings, and hear
what he said unto *she.*

I saw he was fearfully nervous, that in fact he
was suffering pain,
By the way that he fussed with his collar and
poked all the chairs with his cane;
That he blushed; that he would n't look at her,
but kept his eyes fixed on the floor,
And took the unusual precaution of taking his
seat near the door.

He began, "It is — er — er — fine weather, —
remarkable weather for May."
"Do you think so?" said she; "it is raining." — "Oh, so it is raining to-day.
I meant 't will be pleasant to-morrow," he stammered: "er — er — do you skate?"
"Oh, yes!" she replied, "at the season; but
is n't May rather too late?"

The silence that followed was awful: he continued, "I see a sweet dove,"
('T was only an innocent sparrow, but blind are
the eyes of true love,)
"A dove of most beautiful plumage on the top
of that wide-spreading tree,
Which reminds me," — she sighed, — "O sweet
maiden! which reminds me, dear angel, of
thee."

Her countenance changed in a moment; there
followed a terrible pause;
I felt that the crisis was coming, and hastily
dropped on all fours,

In order to see the thing better. His face grew
as white as a sheet,
He gave one spasmodical effort, and lifelessly
dropped at her feet.

She said — what she said I won't tell you. She
raised the poor wretch from the ground.
I drew back my head for an instant. Good
heavens! Oh, what was that sound?
I eagerly peered through the darkness, — for
twilight had made the room dim, —
And plainly perceived it was kissing, — and kiss-
ing not all done by him.

I burst into loud fits of laughter: I know it was
terribly mean,
Still I could n't resist the temptation to appear
for a while on the scene;
But she viewed me with perfect composure, as
she kissed him again with a smile,
And remarked, 'twixt that kiss and the next
one, that "she 'd known I was there all the
while."

May 12, 1871.

LIFE-PRESERVERS.

WHEN Jacques and François had re-
turned from the war,
Their neighbors, delighted to see them once
more,
Sat sipping their toddy around.
"You wonder," said Jacques, "that you see me
survive.
Let 's drink to the one thing which keeps men
alive,
'T is *presence of mind,* I have found.

"When all of my comrades had fallen, one day,
And I, left alone, was still fighting away,
Surrounded by heaps of the dead,
A shell from the English came shrieking along;
It deafened my ears with its horrible song;
I saw it would burst near my head.

"I watched it while coming, and, jumping round
spry,
I bit off the fuse, and then let it go by;
Its wind tore the clothes off my body.
In all sorts of dangers, we old soldiers find
The great life-preserver is *presence of mind.*
Come, off with your glasses of toddy."

"And I," cried François, "have a toast to pro-
pose.
A story shall back it. Fill up! and here goes
The like of this never was seen.
One night, after seven days' fighting, half dead,
All worn out and tired, I made up my bed
On top of a large magazine.

"At midnight, a whizzing I heard, and there
fell
And pierced to the powder a big Russian shell;
There rose up great mountains of dirt;
There never was seen an explosion so great.
Of course I was startled; yet, strange to relate,
Not a bone of my body was hurt.

"'T is true, I declare, as I sit here this minute,
My *bed* blew to thunder, but *I was n't in it!*
Get ready your glasses of toddy!
In battles and blow-ups, and things of that kind,
There 's one thing still better than presence of mind.
Come, here goes to *absence of body!*"

December 20, 1867.

A YARN.

IT was an ancient mariner, — like Coleridge's,
I ween, —
His face was bronzed by tropic suns, his form
was gaunt and lean ;
His hair like tangled oakum was, his eye shot
baleful flame;
He used tobacco, and he walked particularly
lame.

I chatted with him on the pier, — he confidential grew,
Descanted on the weather, and then asked me
for a chew;[1]

[1] Author's note : —

A lady critic says this line is coarse, and will not do;
So we'll substitute another, which is proper, though untrue.
Read: "Railed against a nasty storm, he thought was on
the brew."

And, when besought to spin a yarn, this old seafaring man
"Shivered his timbers but he would!" and suddenly began:

"Ten years ago I shipped upon the schooner Mary Jane.
We sailed for Mozambique, in search, ostensibly, of cane;
The fact is, we were pirates, and a bloodier-minded crew
Ne'er raised the black flag at the fore, or floated on the blue.

"Six weeks across the aqueous main our good ship slowly sailed;
Our fores'ls braced, our tops'ls triced, our main-sheet closely brailed.
The wind it blew S. E. by S., there was a chopping sea,
And silently, with wicked eyes, the fishes followed we.

"Blood-red the sun crawled up the east, blood-red he sank from sight;

Blood-red the moon rose, and the stars twinkled
blood-red by night.
Fool that I was to doubt the sign! Oh, triple
dolt and knave!
The purple sea, that rose and fell, was in its
core, a grave!

"For six long weeks we drifted on, we had nor
food nor water;
We ate the cook, we ate the mate, we ate the
captain's daughter.
The sails grew mouldy overhead, — ha! ha! the
fishes laughed, —
We broke into the medicine-chest, and all its
contents quaffed.

"A quart of rhubarb was my share, I made it
last a week;
My messmate Joe drew senna salts, the tears
stood on his cheek;
The captain, who for food had saved six shirts
and one bandanna,
Was forced to wash his victuals down with ipe-
cacuanha.

Oh! how the fishes roared with glee, to see our sorry plight;
The sun ho-ho'd above all day, the moon te-he'd all night.

"Didst ever feel the wolfish fiend, that man 'starvation' calls?
The powder was but sorry food, — far worse the cannon-balls;
But when it came to eating up, *as we did*, the kedge-anchors,
It's not the sort of diet, boy, for which my stomach hankers."

The mariner here paused and sighed. I sought to rise and go.
He held me in an iron grasp, his words were whispered low:

"The captain still had kept the log, — hunger our courage nerved, —
We eagerly devoured it, because — 't had been *preserved.*
The *fig*ure-head was next dispatched; the boat-swain made *wry* faces, —

We bolted him, but he was tough, and bony,
too, in places.

"Our next prey was the cabin-boy,—ah, sir!
you need not stare.
We ate him, not since he was young, but since
his face was *fare.*
The pilot at the tiller stood, and jammed it hard-
a-lee.
(He would have *jam*med it hard-a-port, but
we'd drunk the *port,* you see.)

"We rushed upon him in a mass, with fear his
senses swam;
We tore his grasp from off the helm, and then
ate up the *jam*"—

"Oh, cease, thou ancient mariner!" I cried, in
great dismay.
"It is a silly yarn you spin; give o'er, nor
longer stay.
Behold a quarter for your pains; take it, and
leave the pier."
The antique sea-dog took the coin, and wiped
away a tear;

Then turned, and sadly wandered off. I ne'er have seen him more,
And never want to, — for he was a most confounded bore.

March 1, 1872.

TO MY QUEEN.

LINES WRITTEN AFTER READING WALT WHITMAN.

I.

WHENEVER she comes, I 'm ready to kiss the mud from her rubbers,
Be she large, or small, or middling;
Be she blonde, brunette, black-eyed, blue-eyed, gray-eyed,
Red-haired, yellow-haired, brown-haired, any-haired, banged, or braided, or down her back;
Be her nose Grecian or Roman, African or otherwise;
Be she rich or poor or indigent;
Daughter of banker, butcher, farmer, farrier, poco,
Hearse or horse-car driver, forger, senator, thief, or rag-picker.

II.

Whenever we meet, I shall know her, wherever
the place of our meeting,
Palace, log-hut, or ordinary brick residence,
Horse-car, steam-car, ferry-boat, oyster saloon,
Parker's, or rum-shop ;
At house-raising, wedding, christening, funeral,
or other places too numerous to mention.

III.

Once found, I 'll be willing to serve her till I
wear myself to a skeleton,
Like galley-slave, plantation-nigger, coolie, cash-
boy, maid-of-all-work,
To serve her as boot-black or maker, watchman,
groom, footman, butler,
Undertaker, hair-dresser, corset-maker, dentist,
ladies' maid, or what not.

March 31, 1876.

A BLUE DAY.

AGES ago in my Sophomore glee,
Frisking away in the thick of it,
Full of my songs and laughter free,
I thought 't was the jolliest life that could be;
But now I 'm a trifle sick of it.

It is n't the work, — that 's not so bad,
Now that they give us our pick of it:
It 's this being snubbed by some low-lived cad,
Or quashed with a "public" for some righteous "mad,"
That makes a fellow so sick of it.

Bells in my ears from morning till night, —
That 's the most cursed trick of it, —
Rousing me up in a horrible fright,
Making me swear, — and you know that 's not right:
I am so heartily sick of it!

Marks and the rank-list bother and fret,
  And that 's but a single kick of it:
The fellows are grown quite a desperate set
With crying forever, "Oh, are n't we men yet?"
  They 're all so tired and sick of it!

"Now what 's the reason?" said I, in despair,
  In talking one evening with Dick of it:
"I 'll tell you," said he, "if to know you care, —
We 're spoiling for want of a little fresh air,
  And that 's why we 're all so sick of it.

"Just wait till the doors are opened wide,
  And you 're shoved out in the thick of it,
With only a sheepskin yourself to hide;
And you 'll vow, if they 'd let you once more inside,
  You 'd never again be sick of it."

March 21, 1871.

ATOMS.

GLEANINGS FROM HERODOTUS.[1]

SADYATTES made war on Miletus,
And in tactics he certainly beat us :
Not at houses he 'd strike ;
But chiropodist like,
He cut off the corn from Miletus.

January 17, 1871.

FOR THE CHEMICAL CHILD.

SING a song of acids
Base and alkali,
Four and twenty gases
Baked into a pie ;
When the pie was opened,
Wonderful to say,
Oxygen and nitrogen
Both flew away !

February 9, 1872.

1 N. B. — The verses are not literal enough to serve as a "pony."

MY LADY.

MOROCCO soft that doth inclose
The white whereon my lady goes;
High heels that lift her lips to mine;
And eyelets with a silver shine,—
Fall not, malignant evening dews,
Lest you should wet my lady's shoes!

O purple grape-leaf on her head,
In silken benediction spread,
With wreaths and ribbons, knotted, curled,
The colors of a magic world,—
Oh, weep not, summer rain, upon it,
Lest you should soil my lady's bonnet!

O nameless art that makes her slim,
Laces in which her shoulders swim,
The daring graces that combine
The "Grecian bend's" delirious line,—
Leaves, shun her as you nestle down,
Lest you derange my lady's gown!

Complexest wonder of the time,
Inspirer of my fervid rhyme,
What odds and ends make up the show,
The gracious lady that I know!
Confusion bright of sex and dress, —
To woo is sweet, — but to possess?

January 8, 1869.

LINES.

HOW oft a little kindly thought,
That to some friendly breast should fly,
In action's clumsy cog-wheels caught,
Its home unreached, must sadly die!

For lordly pride, or selfish sin,
Or some unkind ill-nurtured doubt,
Will shut the little cherub in,
And let their own rude demons out.

Or, from the cradle ere he springs,
Propriety, all staid and stupid,
Will cut away the infant's wings,
Lest fools should take him for a cupid.

So in the crowded heart he lies,
'Mid thoughts of baser birth to smother;
Or lonely from his home he flies,
And has not strength to find another.

But, trust me, dear, the time shall come,
  Either in this world or a better,
When the poor boy shall find a home,
  And grow new wings, and burst each fetter.

Then shall we know our friends aright,
  And stand astonished as they meet us,
At the good thoughts, long kept from sight,
  That rise all angel-like to greet us.

December 21, 1866.

AN EPISODE.

IT was the plump conductor,
  On the Friday-night last car,
Who told the tale I now rehearse,
  When proffered a cigar.

But I must first premise that he
  Used language rather queer,
Which I have changed as best I could,
  And keep his meaning clear: —

"One night, as we were driving in,
  A youngish student fellow
Got on my car dressed up to kill, —
  Hat, new; tie, blue; gloves, yellow.

"Another chap got on with him;
  They both took seats together,
And rattled on about the night,
  Which threatened nasty weather.

"Discussed the Bostons' latest match,
Touched on the Mystic races;
Lydia's burlesque troupe criticised,
Praised various pretty faces.

"And, after they 'd exhausted all
Their stock of sporting knowledge,
The swell one, he began to tell
About his life at College.

"Good gracious! What yarns he did spin
About his various actions;
Two maiden ladies near him turned
To virtuous petrifactions.

"He said he 'd cut six times that week;
And, in one recitation,
Thrown pebbles at the tutor, to
The students' delectation.

"He said (he was a Sophomore),
The night before, out hazing,
He 'd held a Freshman o'er a grate,
In which a fire was blazing.

"He told about a ballet-girl
To whom he 'd sent a letter,
Likewise a bang-up old bouquet,
For which he was a debtor.

"'It cost me fifteen dollars, but
I 'll just write home and say it
Was spent for books, and my old man
Will pony up and pay it.'

"And then he was a-gushing on
About a punch he 'd given,
Where, just to see who 'd drink the most,
The fellows all had striven;

"And how they 'd had a jolly row,
Black eyes, ensanguined noses:
And how (to use his language, sir)
He got as tight as Moses.

"When a man who 'd sat just next to him
(His face was rather hidden),
And in the shade had listened to
These stories all unbidden,

"Now slowly turned round in his seat,
And caught this student's vision,
And gave him just one look that was
Half rage and half derision.

"You should have seen that student's face:
Were n't he astonished? rather!
The man who 'd heard each word he 'd said,
Just think, sir, was *his father!*

"I heard as how that student caught,
When he got home that night,
The most all-fired — Here we are!
Mind the last step! All right!"

The car went on; we 'd reached the Square;
I walked off to my room;
And still that festive student's fate
To me is wrapped in gloom.

October 13, 1871.

PART II.

SONG.

WHEN visions of her face come o'er me,
 Of her sweet face so far away,
I say what lovers said before me,
 What lovers will forever say:
That flowers bloom sweeter for her being,
That birds sing sweeter for her seeing,
That grass is greener, skies more blue,
That all things take a richer hue.
  Lovers have said these things before:
  Lovers will say them evermore.

O sweet young love, that in all ages
 Bears ever one eternal form!
With lasting youth your oldest pages
 Glow ever, ever fresh and warm.
O dear old story ever young!
Poets have painted, artists sung:

Sure, naught in life is half so sweet ;
Death cannot make you incomplete.
    Lovers have said these things before :
    Lovers will say them evermore.

November 13, 1868.

BY THE RIVER.

THE day was well-nigh done ;
And from his chambers in the west
The rosy-visaged sun
Was earthward looking ere he went to rest.
Under the hemlock's green,
Two mossy rocks between,
We found arranged a quiet, sylvan seat,
Such as old fables rare
Say faun and naiads fair
Build by each river in some cool retreat.

But little thought we then,
Reclining on the soft green sprays,
Of deities or men
Who lived in those ideal days,
Or yet of those to be :
Enough it was that we

Were living in that sweetest, dearest time
    When Love is god supreme,
    And earth and nature beam
With light that cometh from his face benign.

    Then slept the god of day,
But where his blazing wheels had rolled,
    Far down the royal way,
Still hung the dust in clouds of red and gold.
    But near us all was dark,
    Save the lone fire-fly's spark,
A trysting signal through the leafy maze ;
    For Love doth all pervade,
    Insect as well as maid
Guideth the loved one by the torch's blaze.

November 9, 1866.

LONGFELLOW.

POET of the many keys,
Rich are all thy melodies !
Not for serf alone nor king
Is the message thou dost bring ;
Not for sect and not for clan,
But for universal man.
Worthy thou to win the fame
That has gathered round thy name.

Poet of the sunny life,
Naught of discord, envy, strife,
Harshly breaking through thy lays,
Mars the music of thy days.
Like the stream, in tranquil power,
Day by day and hour by hour,
Flows thy gentle life along,
Sweeter than thy sweetest song.

Poet of the silver locks,
Time the thoughtless graybeard mocks ;

But in reverence bends his head
Where the great and noble tread.
Men, too, low and reverent,
Praise the years so wisely spent,
Such the life that thou dost live,
Such the homage we would give.

Poet of the kindly heart,
Better than the classic art
That the Muse has deigned to lend
Every page thy hand has penned,
Is the love which thou hast taught,
By each tender word and thought,
Sprung from other hearts, to twine
Round that loving heart of thine.

Poet of the golden tongue,
Still sing on as thou hast sung,
Through the future, as the past, —
Ever sweeter to the last!
Ere the snow shall fill thy paths,
Bring home many Aftermaths;
Still, as thou hast been so long,
Be our Chrysostom of song!

November 14, 1873.

THE VIOLET CROWN.

Αἱ λιπαραὶ καὶ ἰοστέφανοι Ἀθῆναι. — Pind. *Fr.* 46.

I.

IN the mild autumnal splendor,
When Athena's violet crown,
Royal with the sun's great jewel,
Wrought the soul's complete renewal,
Wrought the soul's complete surrender
Of the thoughts that earth it round ;

II.

By a shadowy cedarn forest,
On the fringe that looketh west,
In the frosty silence standing,
Agonized as one commanding
Grief when stillest and when sorest,
He sought grandly God's grand rest.

III.

All the heavens downward flashing,
Aye compellant of earth's worship,
Drew a prayer from out the branches,
Sighing like a soul that launches
All his hope on surges dashing
Back a broken spar for heirship.

IV.

Slowly through his wounded being
Stole the sad Æolian tone ;
And the music of its nature,
Lighting each heroic feature,
Till he seemed too rapt for seeing,
Mingled his soul with its own.

V.

" Beauty is the utmost border
That my soul can reach toward God,"
(Slow he spoke in ripe conviction) ;
" In thee is no interdiction,
Severing man from nature's order,
Love from love beyond the sod.

VI.

"When thy Godhood shone translucent
In Athena's violet crown,
Bringing low life's utmost blisses
To the level of warm kisses
Of the poets, like pure dew sent
Carmined rose-hearts deep adown,

VII.

"That grand priesthood at thy altars,
Hero lips with truth impearled,
Uttering forth thy high evangel
In the plane-tree's whispering chancel,
Careless of the myth that falters,
Wrought the future of the world.

VIII.

"And though low thine Attic ruin
Lieth hid in cerements cold,
Poets kneel for consecration, —
Masters kneel for coronation
At thy holy shrine, renewing
There the Grecian worship old.

IX.

"Kings of Art and Song's magicians
Know thee for the sole divine;
Into deeds they work their worship
And achieve the Christ-like heirship,
Power to work the great remission
Of the sins of human kind.

X.

"Dante's clear eyes caught thy glory
When far off thy coming shone;
Loveless Tasso, through kings' laughter,
And their smiting scorn thereafter,
Keeping in Song's oratory
Deathless fires before thy throne, —

XI.

"Keats, thy chosen, by recoiling
Of his whole soul from earth lust,
By that absolute submission
Of his whole life to the vision
Of the ideal, and the foiling
Of his future in the dust, —

XII.

"All our highest, all our holiest
    Bear thy chrism on their brows ;
    And they build by thought and action
    Temples whose sublime attraction
  Shall grow ever, till the lowliest
    There shall higher life espouse.

XIII.

"Art is sleeping by thy chalice,
    Thought and music climb alone,
    While life moans with fierce gold fever,
    And the common man had liefer
  Nero's sensual golden palace
    Than the patriarch's dreaming stone.

XIV.

"Let me fight no more the duel
    Of earth's joy with heaven's frown, —
    Let me serve thee where my place is,
    Till once more in yon blue spaces,
  Royal with the sun's great jewel,
    Men see Athens' violet crown."

XV.

Quiet grew life's subtile passion,
  Touched by Beauty's breath divine ;
  Not Jehovah's, not another's,
  He passed forth among his brothers
All his earnest life to fashion
  For her crimson-veinéd shrine.

October 16, 1874.

THEE.

THY sweet name speaks in all I hear,
  Thy face alone I see;
My very life from day to day
  Is but a dream of thee.

Whate'er has power to charm my sight,
  From thee its beauty took;
Thy shadow in my pathway lies,
  Thine image in the brook.

Each dew-drop of the morning proves
  A mirror of thy face,
And every blossom at my feet
  Has something of thy grace.

The blackbird from the thicket calls,
  The robin from the tree;
Their songs were ne'er before so sweet,
  As since they sing of thee.

Though absent, still I feel thee near
  In all that meets my eye,
And ever comes the thought of thee
  From field and wood and sky.

January 22, 1875.

THE BELLS OF VENICE.

FROM the stately Campanilé, from the convents far and wide,
From Saint Marco's, from Saint Mary's, o'er the Adriatic's tide,
From the old Armenian cloister, out upon the broad lagoon,
Sound the brazen tongues announcing evening, — come, alas! too soon.

Oh, how rich their cadence swelling, ebbing like the ocean-tide —
Tuneful waves that in the twilight 'neath the marble bridges glide —
Bearing with it thoughts of incense, thoughts of altars draped in white,
Laden with the vesper music soothing evening into night.

Heavy with the breath of angels breathing out
their evening prayer,
Freighted with the sun's last blushes fading from
the evening air ;
Calling in responsive echoings, from the secrets
of the heart,
To its soft and plaintive music, harmony in every
part.

'T is a wondrous, golden music streams from
Venice' brazen bells,
Like the honeyed speech of Nestor, as the olden
poet tells ;
'T is the mem'ry of its freedom in the halcyon
days of yore,
Wafted from the fallen Venice, Hadria's mighty
queen no more.

April 11, 1873.

AD LAURUS CUPIENTEM.

THE glorious bards I love so well!
  A bard I too would be;
Their touch could wake the chorded shell,
  Why wakes it not for me?
Their soaring thoughts my thought pursues
  Through every lofty line;
Does fate the nobler gift refuse,
  Or may their art be mine?

Ah, patience! 'T was the god at play
  That stretched those chords of gold
Across the reptile's shell that lay
  Sluggish and dumb and cold.
Patience! and if the Muses keep
  Their heavenly fires for thee,
One day thy soul from darkest sleep
  Shall spring to ecstasy.

October 2, 1868.

FOREBODINGS.

THE winds and the waves are wailing,
  And the night is full of tears;
And over my spirit forebodings
  Are borne from the coming years.

I fear for the child heart in me,
  With its oneness of faith and sight,
Lest the glow of its strong endeavor
  Go out in the passionate night.

I fear for the swift feet running
  Full speed through the morning dew,
Lest they fail in the arid race-course,
  With the goal, unwon, in view.

I fear lest the motive for striving
  Is perishing in the strife;
I fear lest the glory of living
  Is darkening in the Life.

I fear, and in tears I shiver,
  At the feet of coming years;
The winds and the waves are wailing,
  And the night is full of tears.

March 11, 1873.

TU DESINE TIMERE.

FROM beyond the tears and the darkness,
  From over the wild, sad sea,
Let the cheer of thy brothers' battle
  Ring back, gallant soul, to thee!

Still on through the midnight of passion,
  Let the star of thy young faith guide;
For we count the hours till we see thee
  In manhood's ranks at our side.

Our ears are set for the ringing
  That heralds thy dew-gemmed feet:
Come, brother! our mail weighs heavy;
  Our nerves wax faint in the heat.

Strive on! for the goal looms nearer
  To us in the strife ahead;
Live on! for our armies are thinning, —
  Our brave and our lovely are dead.

Then, when ocean and night wail dreary,
  Let the breath of the coming years
Show a flash of the red-cross banner, —
  Waft the call of thy brothers' cheers!

March 21, 1873.

ANACREONTIC.

WHEN the Muses made wine, as mythologists tell,
They dipped a few drops from their own sparkling well;
On Helicon's water dropped Venus a kiss;
And Cupid, her son, stirred it in with his fist.

So now when the poet his mind would inflame,
He drinks of the wine which from Helicon came;
Straightway Aphrodite leans over his pen,
And the dead Muses live in his verses again.

May 26, 1871.

THE FLIGHT OF THE SWALLOWS.

TELL me, swallows, southward flying,
  As the autumn leaves are dying,
And the sunsets of September
  Paint in crimson all the west, —
In the joy of your returning,
Does there never come a yearning
For the days now gone forever,
  When, within your downy nest,
You from all the stir of travel
  Were at rest?

In the thoughts of your to-morrow
Comes there never one with sorrow,
Of the wakening flood of spring-tide,
  When you first became our guests?
Of the dreamy days of summer,
When each wee, half-fledged new-comer
Found in you a tender parent,
  Serving gladly its behests;

Flying far, on wing untiring,
  In your quests?

Does there never fall a sadness
O'er your hopes of coming gladness,
As the visions, born of memory,
  Bring the yesterdays again?
Or do you, the fled forgetting,
Not a single joy regretting,
Fly to pleasures yet untasted,
  Undisturbed by brooding pain;
Counting not a loss, the vanished, —
  But a gain?

O ye volatile air-swimmers!
As the dusk around me glimmers,
I am wishing for a hopeful
  Resignation like to yours:
For a heart which shall not borrow
From its buried past a sorrow,
But look gladly to its future
  For a solace that endures;
For the balm of time that every
  Grieving cures.

In my memory's glass beholden,
There lie summer days, so golden,
That their recollection seemeth
  As of evanescent dreams;
And, amid the many faces
That my fond remembrance traces,
There is one, above all others,
  That brings sunshine where it gleams;
And my mind with poignant anguish
  Straightway teems.

Oh, the rapture of her smiling,
All my loving soul beguiling,
And the sweet, delirious fervor
  That my heart nursed in its core!
But, alas! the smiles have vanished;
From the flowery path I 'm banished
Which I thought to tread with her,
  My love, my life, for evermore!
And the rosy hours of happiness
  Are o'er.

And I sit and watch you, swallows,
And my heart your flying follows,

And I long to journey with you
  To some southern land more blest;
Where my soul may cease its yearning
For a lost love, ne'er returning, —
May be reconciled to viewing
  My affliction for the best:
May, in peaceful, rapt oblivion,
  Find its rest.

December 20, 1872.

HORACE.

OUR Horace lived for love: his soul was one
That dwelt not separate from the haunts of men,
Like some far-distant star whose flight has been
Far from its brothers, and whose light has shone
To 'lume its own misguided course alone.
For he was human, and his heart in tune
With all Life's various melody; his gloom
Was gladder than the joy most men have known.
The many voicéd laughter of the earth
Sang ever in his ears; and his delight
Was a soft eye in woman, like the night
To which his own Italian skies gave birth.

And oft there steal a blush of brimming wine
And glow of purple grapes across the page,
Like morning o'er the waves. Gone is his age:
Yet oft I feel his warm hand clasped in mine.

April 1, 1873.

NEWPORT.

THE rain had ceased: fierce howled the wind,
And ragged clouds went hurrying by;
The screaming gull wheeled in his flight,
And shone against the leaden sky.

I walked upon the barren cliffs;
And under, in the hollow caves,
I heard the giant breakers' roar,
And ebb and flow of angry waves.

I looked upon the smooth, wet beach,
Which glistened, as a single ray
Burst from behind the thunder-cloud,
And edged with gold the gloomy gray.

I saw, half-buried in the sand,
And dark with sea-weed covered o'er,
A battered wreck, a shattered hulk,
And three worn head-stones on the shore.

January 17, 1873.

PRAYER OF THE RIVER GOD TO APHRODITE.

COME, goddess with the golden hair,
And tender eyes divinely fair,
And lips from which of old I drew
All unreproved the honey dew, —
With brow as white as driven snow,
And voice more musical and low
And sweeter far than lute or song, —
Why should you stay from me so long?
Can act of mine have done you wrong?

Still linger you afar to rove
By fount and stream through Ida's grove?
Or do your feet delight to roam
Across the blue sea's crested foam,
While all the bright and sunny isles
Bask in the summer of your smiles, —
Cythera with its myrtle shades,
Or Cyprus with its Paphian maids?

Or is it Eryx now invites
Your presence by her temple rites,
Close by the long Sicilian strand?
Where'er it be, — that favored land
That holds you now in grove or glen, —
Come to your lover's arms again!

Ah! well can I recall when first
Upon my sight, enraptured, burst
The vision of your love-lit eyes,
Your bosom shaken oft with sighs,
The glory of your curls that rolled
Adown your neck their wealth of gold!
How did the heart within me melt,
When tenderly you came and knelt
Beside my cool and grassy brink,
Where the tall deer delights to drink!
The birds sang carols in the trees,
And lightly sighed the passing breeze,
While silently beneath your tread
Each floweret bent its tiny head.
The very sunbeams felt the charm;
And, stealing o'er each rounded arm,

Kissed lip and cheek and brow that shone
Far whiter than the Parian stone,
Or than the stately swans that glide
Serenely down my silver tide.

But slow and sad the days have passed,
And weary are the weeks since last
My eyes were with your beauty blest.
And now the heart sinks in my breast;
Yet, half despair, half hope, I yearn,
And wait in vain for your return.
Nor I alone: all Nature, too,
Longs to behold your face anew, —
Your lips more sweet than ruby wine,
The very blossoms droop and pine,
And all their fragrance closely hoard.
The grass is withered on the sward.
The olive, that above me weaves
Its branches, drops its yellowing leaves,
And casts to earth, unripe, its fruit.
While in the boughs the birds, all mute
And moveless, perch the whole day long,
Too sad alike for flight or song.

And far away, in echo faint,
I hear the ring-dove's lonely plaint,
Like me, with woe disconsolate,
Over its loved and absent mate.
More sweet than mine its mellow moan:
Alike our grief, — that Love has flown.

Then, Aphrodite, come and kiss
My lips, and thrill my heart with bliss!
Bring back once more Love's sunny hours,
And bless with me both birds and flowers.

March 6, 1874.

REVERIE.

SEE this fair smoke-wreath, from my pipe ascending,
In perfect poise drift slowly through the air;
E'en as I gaze, the gentle union ending,
It melts away, yet leaves a fragrance there.

We met and parted; but the few short hours
Which held our hearts in happy union here,
Have thrown a fragrance o'er this life of ours,
Which sweet shall linger through each after year.

Our college life is but a sudden meeting,
As sudden parting, and we haste away;
Yet something gather from these moments fleeting,
Which we shall keep until our dying day.

We meet and part on earth, our brief existence
  One grain upon eternity's vast shore ;
But Love, the gift of God, shall have subsistence
  When Time hath faded in the evermore.

December 21, 1866.

CLASS ODE.

I.

LIKE the thousands before us, we gather to-day,
  And with beauty in blossom and gem;
And we march on the world as high-hearted as they,
  To forget, be forgotten, like them.
Forget thee, my brother? forgotten by thee?
  Alma Mater, *thy* blessing forgot?
Oh, dry with the dryness of ashes will be
  The heart that remembereth not!

II.

Give thy hand to me, brother! Farewell must be said.
  There is bitterness Love would prolong:
There are prayer for the living and praise of the dead;
  There are sorrow and promise and song.

Alma Mater, God bless thee ! Dear Mother,
    adieu !
  On our tongues are hurrah ! and alas !
'T is alas ! for the days that will never renew.
  'T is hurrah ! we salute thee and pass.

June 25, 1869.

IN THE ADIRONDACKS.

HOW sweet, from care and study free,
When summer's breath blows warm again,
To leave the busy haunts of men,
The rank salt odors of the sea,
For fragrance of the mountain pine ;
To woo the pensive solitude,
In temples of primeval wood ;
The still-traced Indian paths, to tread ;
To feel the sun more softly shine ;
And when the west is tinted red,
And sunset light o'er earth is spread,
To bathe as if in baths of wine !
Unbroken by the miller's wheel,
Broad rivers glide through rows of trees,
With murmurings that never cease ;
While through the waving boughs are seen
The nearer mountains clothed with green,
The distant colored like blue steel.

The lakes at noon are floors of glass,
Painted with wonders at the rim
Of unreal foliage, more true
To life in every form and hue
Than earth's best masters ever drew;
And fleecy clouds that o'er them pass
Repass as in a sky below
So gracefully, we scarcely know
If they be things that fly or swim.
But sweeter still it is, at night,
To see the camp-fire flickering
On huge gnarled trunks and boughs that swing
Within the circle of its light;
Or gaze across the river's breast,
And see upon the farther shore
The birches in the moonlight dressed
Like ghosts of trees; and hear the roar
Of distant rapids, soft, subdued
Into the night's more tranquil mood.

November 14, 1873.

FANCHON.

OH, merry little Cricket, how happily you laugh !
You find a little joy in all that lies upon your way ;
And though your joy be partial, and grief claims the other half,
Though sorrow come to-morrow, you laugh while 't is to-day.

And then, poor little Cricket, how easily you weep !
Fate has been hard to you, dear child, and shown but little rest ;
And you laugh in vain, for tears will stain your lashes when you sleep,
For the secret, fervent, childish love, that glows within your breast.

While a single spark of conscience shines in worldly hearts and cold,
  While a single memory remains of better, purer years,
You shall hold in perfect sympathy with you both young and old,
  Turning all to mirth and sadness with your laughter and your tears.

May 11, 1867.

AN ALPINE DAY.

O BRILLIANT light! O azure sky
O happy fountain, leaping high
With never-varying melody,
To greet the royal day!

Ye sombre summits bathed in mist,
And smiling slopes by sunbeams kissed,
And brooklets trickling toward the tryst
Within the placid bay, —

Your life and splendor gladden me;
Ye fill my heart with ecstasy;
My pulses dance in frolic free,
As in the florid May.

. . . . . .

The sun sails high through cloudy seas;
The shadows shrink beneath the trees;
And faintly sighs the singing breeze
Among the branching pines.

More lightly stir the blades of green,
In drooping tufts of glossy sheen,
Between whose rootlets, all unseen,
 The daisy's head reclines.

And sunlight crowns the terraced swells,
Rising above the narrow dells
In serried beauty, that foretells
 A vintage of red wines.

. . . . . .

The end draws near of daily toil,
The changeless round of dull turmoil ;
And peasant workers of the soil
 Are trooping slowly by.

The jodel rings along the height ;
Flashes of arrowy, amber light,
Flung by the sun in falling might,
 Waver, and wane, and die ;

And, dying, fade behind the hills ;
While the air with sudden coolness fills,
And the heart with quiet pleasure thrills,
 Under the star-lit sky.

May 2, 1873.

THE LIFE AND DEATH OF PIETRO.

ANNO DOMINI 1348.

"AGAIN the light of earth, and the live air,
The uncertain shadows of the midnight moon,
And the great mountains set athwart the East;
And here, here, here, black in the virgin light,
The fragments of the broken crucifix
I broke, while those two yellow shrivelled monks, —
Those four fierce eyes gnawing my peace away, —
Stood with affrighted shoulders, fearful hands,
Recoiling eyes in which black horror gloomed,
Their withered lips blanched by the rising curse,
That leaves God's desolation where they flee.
And then the swoon which I had thought was death.

I had not thought to feel life's pulse again.
How beautiful the light is, and the sky,
Night's shadowy splendor full of tranquil thoughts
And dreams of sweet love's mossy tryst! — O God!
Within an hour loveliness dies for me!
Nor holy ground shall hush my outcast soul, —
O falsest truth! all earth is holy ground
Since first God launched it on the arcs of space
And consecrated every vale and mount
With Beauty that transcends the mystic touch
Of priest-blessed water as God transcends man.
Nature shall watch my uncompanioned grave;
For I have loved her, and have given life
To make her lovely in the eyes of men.
The silent, viny forests ever shook
My soul with worship, and a Grecian joy
Shot all the sunshine through me till I felt
Each throbbing sense hunger and thirst for Life.

Still in my boyhood, 'mong the Apennines,
I sought the flowers of richest fragrance out;
I wandered where the grandest music rose
From ancient forests, climbed the highest peak
To catch the earliest glory of the sun;
Every voluptuous sense made revel wild,
Swift Love upon his golden sandals flew,
Sowing the twilight with his timorous thoughts,
Robbing my sleep to crown me with delight,
Made wakeful as the mateless nightingale,
While all the earth was gay with Eden bloom.
So I passed out into the world of men,
Under the darkness that from Judah rose,
Smothering the light of joy and dowering man
With curses, and an infinite curse at last.
I could not think but that the earth was God's,
That something noble was the base of man,
Since God had made him; Joy was all my Life,
I could not coffin it in daily woe.
I groped in th' dark and groaned, until one day —
I was sixteen that month — in Florence streets

I saw a man burned in the market square;
I saw the monks' scorn-lifted fingers flung —
A-quiver to the tips with malign hate
And cursings showered upon that son of God —
I saw those shrunk and maddened fingers flung
Into his face, and when the crackling flames
Ravished that resolute face from shuddering thought,
I felt the inspiration of the truth
Seize on my stricken soul with eloquent heat,
Transfiguring my life into the hope
And beacon of the world that walks in night.
Art called me to her, and I served my art
With every thought and act of all my hours;
In every painting, golden with the light
And blushing with our most impassioned blood,
I set the naked form of natural joy,
Draped with the richest robes of ideal life.
Love called me to her, and I served my love
With every hope and longing of all hours —
O Beatrice, magnificent in love,

Crowned queen of all the rapture of my
dreams,
How holy was that swift departing Life
Wherein we worshipped God by loving each
The other humanly, and so indeed
Divinely, in the transport and the blush,
The ecstasy of every panting sense
Which is the passion-flower of human joy.
Then fell the blaze of lightning on my path,
My paintings shrivelled in a holy fire,
And holy men dragged my sweet love behind
The hopeless iron of their convent gates.
For lack of her, our boy, in sad neglect,
Unmothered, lingered out a little month
And died before he felt the joy of life.
'T is five years since I stood in Florence
streets,
Five sunny years of joy and art and love,
And now the storm of human hate beats down
My mangled life. Wife, child, and calling
gone,
Left lonely in my death, I 'm still, I 'm cold,
I cry not out against the love of God, —

Men's ignorance hath made them what they
are, —
The world 's gone mad with Christ! But, O
my Art,
Who will reveal the gospel hid in thee,
Beauty's evangel and Earth's holiness,
Our great descent e'en from the loins of God?
Who will display the eloquence of joy,
Remarry the long sundered soul and flesh,
Proclaim the sanctity of every throb
That Nature's impulse quickens in the blood?
O Art, my Art, I thought to clasp thee close,
Even as a bride in my impassioned arms,
And from our union blessed light should spring,
Unsealing the blind eyes of stumbling men.
I 'm palsied now, — oh, this is sorrow's height
To see your loved ones toss in torturing pain,
And know no strength can reach from you to
them!
Earth 's ghostly round me! O thou wondrous
moon,
And pallid fires of the undying stars,
And breath of the warm zephyr, — ye are
gone!

Farewell Delight, sweet Art, and blessed Love,
All form and color of the universe, —
Now 's the swift fateful dawn of the unknown."

March 5, 1875.

MY JEAN.

HAE onie seen my sonsie lass,
  Wi' loe light in her een,
Gae trippin' through the meadow grass, —
  My blythe and bonny Jean ?

Her lips are cherries ripe an' red,
  But sweeter far to taste ;
An', while these puir weak words are said,
  I feel her kiss amaist.

Her cheeks are roses brent an' saft,
  O' blush and beauty fu',
An' mony times hae I an' aft
  Laid mine by hers to woo.

Her dainty han' is white and sma',
  An' aft an' aft again,
Wi' sweet caress an' kiss an' a',
  I 've held it in my ain.

An' aft her curly head has laid
  Its wealth o' gowd to rest,
Wi' naught to hurt or make afraid,
  Upon my willin' breast.

Her laugh is like the wimplin' breuk
  That flaws along the stanes,
But nane can tell how sweet her leuk
  Till they have seen it ance.

Why need I tell you that her arms
  Haud a' my warld between?
Nae ither lass has half her charms,—
  An' hae ye seen my Jean?

June 11, 1875.

IN MAY DAYS.

THE still hours of the afternoon,
The violets' scent, the orioles' song,
The peaches' delicate warm bloom,
The grass that long

Hath borne the promise of the spring,
Alone, in hope, the sweet new grass
O'er which now whitened fruit-trees swing,
And swiftly pass

Blithe birds in their melodious flight
Among calm elms and maples fair,
Whose fresh buds ope in golden light
And southern air, —

The blossomed loveliness of May,
Out of the silence sudden wrought,
Out of long desolate decay
In glory brought ;

O strange May days, unwreathed I bow
  My head before your faultless grace;
I have no single flower that now
    And here finds place.

Unworthy am I among these:
  Strange beings of an unknown world,
The flowers, the birds, the grass, the trees,
    Their lives unfold

In ideal beauty; without flaw
  The best that is in them bears bloom;
And grandly by their unguessed law
    Their forms assume

An utmost loveliness that makes
  The earth a marvellous delight,
Wherein the soul its pleasure takes
    By day and night.

But we, what have our spirits done
  That can with this great work compare?
Or where of men doth anyone
    Such glories wear?

In presence of this perfect May,
  Our incompleteness shames our eyes,
Our barren souls, our bloomless day,
    Where Beauty dies.

Yet from the May great strength doth well,
  Although ourselves we humble thus ;
The same Divinity doth dwell
    In it, in us.

Unerring through the passing years,
  The Spirit shapes its law unguessed ;
The fulfilled hope of all things nears, —
    In this we rest.

October 8, 1875.

"ROCKED IN THE CRADLE OF THE DEEP."

THE sun is shining soft but strong,
The glad waves sing their rippling song;
The freshened breeze,
Across the seas,
Blows merrily along.

Close by the surface, skimming light,
The sea-gulls wing their graceful flight;
And where they lave,
The dancing wave
Flashes with crystals bright.

The wide-spread field of Ocean's blue
Unnumbered folds of canvas strew,
To where its dim
And distant rim
Unites with lighter hue.

Beneath the bow, with deadening sound,
The surging billows ceaseless pound;
While, flashing gray,
The sparkling spray
Is tossed in showers around.

At full length, by the bowsprit's heel,
From Dream-land gentle breaths I feel;
With anthems deep,
The waters sweep
Along the oaken keel.

The voice of sailor heard afar,
The distant creaking of the spar,
The flapping sail,
The swaying brail, —
In music softened are.

The sounds around, the roar below,
To one commingled murmur grow;
Till, lost in sleep,
My slumbers deep
Feel the harmonious flow.

June 21, 1872.

SOUPIR.

A WATERY waste where the wind is blowing;
A cold wind, blowing in sobs and sighs;
A strip of sand, with dry grass growing, —
Above, night falling from leaden skies.

Two, but two, on the sand strip straying,
Pacing its limits up and down;
Loath to linger, but still delaying,
Dreading return to the fading town.

One last kiss of the lips that never,
Never shall touch each other more;
One hand pressure, the last forever, —
Empty and lone is the sandy shore.

A wealth of waves in the sunshine dancing;
A wind that ripples their tops to foam;
A strip of sand in the bright light glancing, —
Above, blue skies where the white clouds roam.

A ship sails out of the harbor slowly,
  With a silent watcher standing a-stern ;
A kerchief waves from a cottage lowly, —
  Ah, God ! the lessons we all must learn.

January 9, 1874.

A SUMMER CLOUD.

BRIGHT summer cloud, how like a dream
Your soft and shadowy tissues seem!
Your form flits through my drowsy sense,
Beguiling all my indolence.
So frail, so fair, so bright you are, —
Now floating near, now lost afar, —
I scarce know if 't was form or thought
That in my soul your image wrought.

Far out upon your airy flight,
On fleecy pinions dipped in light,
Your fairy shape appears to me
A ship upon the azure sea.
Should I essay to paint a star, —
How faithless earthy pigments are!
To paint your radiance divine,
I fain a sunbeam would confine.

So frail, ah me ! and fleeting too,
How like an earthly joy are you !
At first a thing of beauty there,
And then you vanish into air ;
At first a rapture past control,
And then a void within the soul.
I cannot brook your absence so,
My song must end if you must go.

May 28, 1875.

PLAYING KITTEN.

HAVE you seen a kitten play with a ball?
She clutches it tight in her sharp little claws,
Tosses it up and then lets it fall;
Rolls it away, and after a pause,
Brings it again to her side; with a spring,
Bounds far from it with motion active,
Yet ne'er, for an instant, loses the thing: —
Oh! a kitten playing is very attractive.

Just so a maiden plays with my heart: —
A moment she holds it caught in her smiles,
Then seems to forget me and turns apart;
And, when I am almost freed from her wiles,
Calls me back with a glance so sweet
That only her in the world I see,
And again lie captive before her feet,
Though I know she is playing kitten with me.

November 12, 1869.

SONG.

MY heart has left the Muses' seat, —
  Her song but half begun;
And, wandering at thy side, my feet
  Forget fair Helicon.

For me no more its verse divine
  Shall mystic Delphi tell;
Thine eyes shall be mine only shrine,
  Thy lips mine oracle.

No marvel, then, that all my song, —
  If verse for chant or lyre, —
Henceforth to thee alone belong,
  Since thou dost both inspire.

June 11, 1875.

A MAY-FLOWER.

I.

"WHAT fitter emblem could love send?"
I mused,
Kissing my blossom tenderly;
True flowers are sweet and frail: I only said,
"How sweet, how strong her love for me!"

We question not of spring-time, "Will it
come?"
With childhood's faith, "Next year," we say,
And wait in dreamy patience, while the long
Still winter days wear slow away.

A trust so perfect rounded all my love,
And held beyond its circling pale
The lightest doubt; such faith could never
look
To days when love's sweet grace should fail.

II.

Full well I mark the south wind blowing through
The days, unloosing winter's hold;
Nor miss the robin's song, rich as his plumes
O'erlapping into crimson fold.

Ah, waiting heart! these months shall never bring
Thy lover's token unto thee;
Oh, dying heart! Oh, cruel wildwood flowers!
To bloom, and she is false to me.

One year! — it seemed so long ere, with the sun,
Would turn its blossoms to the sky;
Perhaps 't is long to wait a May-flower's birth;
Ah, God! 't is short for love to die.

March 16, 1869.

YOU KISSED ME.

YOU kissed me in my dream, love;
  Your face lay close to mine;
Your breath played with my glossy curls
  As zephyrs with the vine:
The hot blood rushed into my face,
  That told my joy too plain;
You saw it, and, with wild delight,
  You pressed my lips again.

My poor heart beat against its walls,
  As if it wished to fly
Above the common thoughts of earth
  To those of love's bright sky.
I asked you why we could not have
  Through life such heartfelt bliss;
You looked, yet uttered not a word,
  But answered with a kiss.

You left me then; and, as I saw
  You disappear from sight,
I woke, and found my lips were kissed
  By beams of morning light.
I sighed to think 't was but a dream,
  But sighed, alas! in vain;
And now I long for you to kiss
  Me in my dreams again.

May 11, 1866.

DESECRATION.

"Earth 's crammed with heaven,
And every common bush on fire with God."

I WANDERED by a shore, through fragrant bowers
Of mid-May locust-blossoms creamy white,
Until the closing petals of the flowers
Foretold the coming night.

Rich colors drifted o'er the sunset sea,
And sudden on a passing ship they shone:
A gorgeous dream of orient alchemy,
The splendid shape sailed on.

The deep dyes slowly paled; a softer hue
(Delicate opal and faint amethyst)
Over the lustrous shadows lightly flew,
And the far islands kissed.

"Holy are altar stairs, but holier far,"
Thought I, "this purple stain of dying day;
Holy was Israel's temple, but a star
Showed where the Saviour lay.

"O blind, blind worshippers, who, awestruck, kneel
Where old cathedrals their hoar stones uplift,
What treasure doth that aged gloom conceal?
Behold God's primal gift, —

"The garden, and the forest-fringéd shore;
The ancient sunset-arches, jewel-bright;
The waveless ocean's still, transparent floor,
Inlaid with rainbow light.

"With heads unbowed, and hearts unlifted up,
Ye look off to yon island's silver edge;
With rough-shod feet ye crush the violet's cup, —
O wanton sacrilege!

"Beauty is visible love, is God's love met
E'en face to face, howe'er His truth grows dim;
An aureole of glory round us set
To show our birth from Him.

"With reverence, O my brothers, look above!
Kneel lowly by the white sands of the sea.
Forgive us, God, that symbols of thy love
We pass by carelessly!"

May 1, 1874.

THE BONNIE WILD ROSEBUD THAT GREW ON THE BRAE.

AFTER THE SCOTCH.

O MONIE braw blossoms are bloomin' alang
The burnie's green side, and the heather amang;
But awa' wi' them a', for there 's nane I lo'e mae
Than the bonnie wild rosebud that grew on the brae.

For, when Jamie pu'd it and gied me to wear,
He kissed it, as sweetly it breathed frae my hair,
An' vowed there was never a lovelier ae
Than the bonnie wild rosebud that grew on the brae.

O' lassies besides me, he vowed there was nane
He lo'ed, but would love me forever alane,
An' he wad na forget, howe'er far he might gae,
That bonnie wild rosebud that grew on the brae.

I gied him my lo'e an' a kiss, an' he said,
"Oh, wear that sweet rosebud the day that we wed!
For though it should wither, yet nane I 'll lo'e mae
Than the bonnie wild rosebud that grew on the brae."

An' now he 's awa' to be gatherin' gear,
But he will na be gane frae me owre a year,
An' then I shall wear on a kindlier day
The bonnie wild rosebud that grew on the brae.

Then let the gay simmer her braw blossoms strew

On the bank o' the burnie or owre the green
knowe,
Sin' Jamie best lo'es it, far sweeter than thae
Is the bonnie wild rosebud that grew on the
brae.

April 30, 1875.

THE WATERS.

FALLS the rain within the valleys,
  Bending through the swelling hills;
Falls the rain within the forests,
  Filling full the flowing rills,

As they dance and sparkle downward,
  In a wild and winding race,
Mingling all their giddy whirlings
  In the river's calmer grace.

While it sweeps, with curves majestic,
  To the grand and solemn main,
Whispering to the land in passing,
  Murmuring a deep refrain.

This the thunderous ocean hearing,
  Roaring o'er its shifting strands,
  Catches and with blows resounding
Beats the rhythm on the sands.

April 12, 1872.

THE BLUE AND THE GRAY.

THE fight had ceased, and o'er the field of
 slaughter
Came slowly down the night,
To cover with her veil the scene of carnage,
Too sad for mortal sight.

Beside a brook which yesterday ran sparkling
Athwart its pebbly bed,
But now, impeded with the dead and dying,
Flowed sluggish on and red,

Beneath a willow's weak and shattered branches,
Like a close mourning veil
That hides the sad tears of some weeping
 mother,
Sad tears of no avail,

The pale moon shining on their upturned faces,
Close side by side there lay

Two soldiers of the fierce contending legions, —
The blue beside the gray.

Two college chums were they; but when stern Sumter
Sent forth th' alarum gun
That roused a nation to fierce strifes and conflicts, —
Armed father against son,

They quarrelled — parted. Each made haste to answer
His party's call to fight;
Each echoing from his heart the patriot's motto,
I battle for the right.

Here they had met, here death had struck them, bringing
Back with that stroke the love
That, dimmed a moment 'mid life's toils and struggles,
Would brighter burn above.

Around lay thickly piled the dead and dying,
Friend — foe — in one sad heap;

The conflict's frown still rested on their fore-
heads,
Their eyes still glared in sleep.

But on the faces of those two fair sleepers
Lay that sweet smile of peace
Which God sends down to bless the good, the
righteous,
That peace which ne'er shall cease.

October 11, 1872.

ODE.

CLASS SUPPER, '69.

OH, bright and sweet the hour we meet!
  Our festal rites begin!
Fill up, fill up the crystal cup,
  Drop friendship's pearl therein!
For us the truth of love and youth,
  The grape-vine's purple gush;
For us, the fairest wreath of fame,
  The maiden's modest blush!

A richer pearl than Egypt's Queen
  Dissolved in Cyprian wine;
See how it tints the fragrant draught,
  See how its bubbles shine;
We leave behind the burdened mind,
  By weighty cares perplexed;
The mirthful bowl these years console,
  And beauty crowns the next.

December 11, 1866.

ELAINE.

ON SEEING ROSENTHAL'S PAINTING.

FAST at the stern the servant, dumb and old,
Stands, guiding with still oar the lonely boat,
That towards some dim shore ever seems to float,
While far away behind the skies are gold.

In sable garb, his features blank with woe,
He seems like him who in the dark lake dips
His blade, and takes the obol from dead lips, —
The gloomy pilot of the shades below.

Fair is the form he watches from above,
That, queen-like, lies upon a couch bedeckt,
Which silken casings overhead protect.
From one hand droops the lily of lost love;

And one upon her breast, all cold and white,
Enfolds the letter which, with feeble breath, —
The tale of love whose only prize was death, —
She bade her brothers in her own words write.

Her face, upturned, with sweet but sad light seems,
In her bright hair that floods the coverlet,
Like a pure pearl in golden collet set, —
A face to live in every gazer's dreams.

For who has not, with cold heart, flung away
Some proffered faith, some trust bestowed unsought,
Whose calm, dead face erelong will haunt his thought
With vain regret o'er what is lost for aye?

That love that longed, so full of grace and truth,
To lay her hand in his and guide his choice,
But which he thrust aside, will find a voice,
Even though dead, to shame his thoughtless youth.

That high Ideal that might else have won
His love and worship, if he had not been
Bound to some Guinevere of darling sin,
With silent lips will say, Undone, undone!

Alas! to every life too soon will come, —
The slow barge floating o'er the refluent tide, —
A dead, forgotten love, across the wide,
Dim waste of waves, with oarsman sad and dumb.

Then all the baubles that have charmed our eyes
Will sink like lead beneath that silent bark,
Which seeks dim shores, o'er billows drear and dark, —
And far behind will seem the golden skies!

February 19, 1875.

HAWTHORNE.

HIS life was like a summer cloud,
  Half gold, half gloom, in hue,
That far above the thoughtless crowd
  Floats through the ether blue.

With some deep mystery concealed,
  It moves serene and slow;
A shadow falls o'er vale and field,
  And marks its place below.

Men call it beautiful; none dream
  How much it lends the day;
But all the fields more lonely seem
  When it has passed away.

February 20, 1874.

SONG.

"'T is not the singing o' the bird."

I.

'TIS not the singing o' the bird,
  Nor burnie roaring free,
That makes the merry month o' May
  The time o' spring to me;
    For were it winter cauld and drear,
      And snaw-clad every tree,
    If I but ken that Jennie's near
      'T is the spring-time to me.

II.

'T is not the blooming o' the rose,
  Nor humming o' the bee,
That makes the leafy month o' June
  The simmer-time to me;

For were it in the winter cauld,
  And snaw-clad every tree,
If Jennie's hand I only hold
  It 's the simmer-time to me.

III.

Were surly Winter frae the year
  To take four times his share,
And rob the other seasons quite,
  I' m sure I wad na care;
    For if my Jennie lo'es me weel,
      And if she constant be,
    The spring-time and the simmer-time
      Will never go frae me.

January 15, 1867.

BEATRICE DI CENCI.

"That perfect mirror of pure innocence."—*Shelley.*

HOW sad yet strangely sweet thy face,
So free from every shade and trace
Of beauty cold and commonplace!

What mingled love and woe intense
Breathe forth a silent eloquence,
That speaks alike to soul and sense!

The inward purity that stole
Forth from thy tried but faithful soul,
Bright as a martyr's aureole,

Around thy features seems to shine,
Making the artist's work divine;
And adding unto every line

A grace and beauty, far apart
From the mere classic charm of art, —
A lustre beaming from the heart.

Oh, who can gaze with tearless eyes
Upon the grief that hidden lies
In sweet but ill-concealed disguise

Within thy half-averted look?
Pity itself long since forsook
The heart that can, unpitying, brook

The sorrow, the reproach, that haunts
Thy mute but all-expressive glance,
And saddens thy fair countenance.

As men guessed from thy face too well
That awful secret, which a spell
Of shame and pride forbade to tell;

Whose cursed weight forever hung
About thy soul; which ne'er was wrung
In words from thine unwilling tongue, —

So now thy sad romance we seek
From thy hushed lips and crimson cheek, —
A tale that words can never speak.

Thanks be to those who won from men
The justice they denied till then!
And one with pencil, one with pen,

Have sought thy story to reveal;
And, taking from thy lips the seal,
Have taught mankind to see, and feel

A scorn and loathing deep for him
Who, when his eyes were old and dim,
Filled up his cup unto the brim

With crimes that strike the world aghast,
And make men, gazing on the past,
Thank Heaven that History fades at last! —

A righteous, bitter hate for those
Who persecuted thee as foes, —
A sympathy with all thy woes.

Guido and Shelley! — at their feet
The world has knelt and caught the beat
Of thine own heart, so pure and sweet,

And, looking in thine eyes, has seen
The innocence that dwelt within;
And judged thee free from that foul sin

Which popes and powers, unkind, unjust,
Upon thy guileless soul had thrust.
Till now the world reveres thy dust,

And, but to make amends, would kiss
The sod where its own prejudice
Laid thy fair form, sweet Beatrice!

April 22, 1873.

SEMPER RESURGENS.

THE storm wind has passed with its echoes
  Of on-coming loss and woe,
And the stainless stars of midnight
  Flash down on the drifted snow.

I hear the low breezes murmur,
  Like thoughts of the shadowy trees,
And my heart is filled with the music
  Of unheard melodies.

Old yearnings of love and lost longings,
  That arise from lonely pain,
Like songs from the twilight ocean,
  Are thrilling my life again.

I feel the glow of love's passion
  Enkindle my ardent veins,
Like wine of the sacrament cleansing
  My soul of its manifold stains.

It transfigures the past, and the legends
  My losses have written for me,
Like odors of violets withered,
  On the breath of midnight flee.

I know, though its idols were broken,
  It lived in the lonely years,
Though the silence of sorrow chilled it,
  And the touch of bitter tears.

I know that our love cannot perish,
  It blends with our life its light,
As the stainless starlight mingles
  Fore'er with the dreary night.

January 23, 1874.

AUTUMN LEAVES.

THE leaves are all abloom with red,
  All dancing though they 're dying.
Like happy butterflies, the wind
  Now sets them all a-flying.

The gay is mingled with the sad, —
  The saddest oft are gayest;
Prone leaf, thou, on thy little page,
  The book of Life portrayest.

October 22, 1875.

CREPUSCULUM.

THE restful twilight hour has come,
  The sweetest of the day.
The merry laugh, the joke and song,
  The clicking of croquet,

And all the far-off busy hum
  Betokening eventide,
Come wafted upward on the breeze,
  And through the casement wide.

The night-hawk, circling far above,
  Is screaming loud and shrill;
The thrush has sung his vesper hymn,
  The robins all are still.

Just through the tops of yonder trees
  The moon begins to show, —
Now bright, now dim, as in the breeze
  The boughs wave to and fro.

The ponderous bells in distant towers
  Peal forth the hour of eight;
And through and through the soft spring air
  Their tones reverberate.

April 22, 1873.

LITERATURE.

THE sea where authors trembling launch
their barks,
A treacherous sea, inviting to the eye
Of youth ambitious, gazing from the shore
Upon the shining tide. He builds his toy,
And ventures it among the sunlit drops
That sparkle on the surface of the swell.
He might a lesson from the bubbles learn:
They smile and dance and die. So may his
hopes.
The caverns of the deep are stored with wrecks,
And 'mid the ribs of many a hope-sped bark
Nameless sea monsters sport in heedless play.
Unwisely, thought he, tempt the mid-sea storms,
The youth is free to coast along the shore.
He may to some small port a cargo bear,
Welcome and full of cheer; and, if one heart
Beats quicker for a humble thought of his,
He has done well to launch his modest lay.

March 5, 1869.

AFTER SUNSET.

I.

ODORS of pine woods,
Scent of the sea,
Perfume of roses,
Wafted toward me,
Breezes that linger,
Fireflies that roam,
White wavelets plashing
Their monotone,
Shadowy elm-trees,
Gray-limbed and tall,
Light of the soft moon,
Clasping it all, —
Though the great sun be slain,
These still remain.

II.

When the great sunset
  Blazed through the west,
Startling all eyes with
  Grandeur unguessed,
Smiting with glory
  Sky and the sea,
"What more," I cried out,
  "Is there for me?"
Slowly its beauty
  Faded away,
Crimson to amber,
  Amber to gray,
Till, as some hero's
  Funeral pyre
Falleth and sends up
  Fierce flakes of fire,
Fell the sun, spark by spark,
  Into the dark.

III.

Lo, but about me,
  Fair on all sides,

Leaving me never,
  Beauty abides.
I hear her calling
  Out of the night, —
"I am eternal,
  I, thy delight;
Though the sun vanish.
  I am still fair;
Though darkness cometh,
  I am still there.
Serve me and trust me,
  That is thy scope;
Cling to me, love me,
  That is thy hope.
Out of the Future
  Cometh an Hour
Viewless and nameless,
  Armed with dread power;
Bringing the ending,
  Its dull strokes call
Thy life from selfhood
  Into the All;
Then thou shalt perish,
  But, when thou 'rt gone,

In me eternal
  Thy life lives on."
I hear her calling,
  Out of the night;
I hear her calling,
  Her, my delight.
Who obeys not the voice
  That bids rejoice?

February 18, 1876.

MADRIGAL.

WHERE shall I look for thee? where shall
I find thee?
Seek thee before me, or seek thee behind me,—
Turn to the Eastward or turn to the West,
Fly to the North or the South to be blest?
Pity my longing, and smile on my fervor!
Wilt thou reveal thyself clad in the armor,
Prithee, of Venus or wisest Minerva?
Give me some token, my beautiful charmer!

Why dost thou linger? what cause may delay
thee?
Hasten to meet me, fair stranger, I pray thee!
Soon may I melt at the sight of thy charms,
Clasped, at the touch of our lips, in thine arms.
Hasten to meet me! Come, sweet moment
fated,

Woo the young bud of my hope into blossom:
Then shall the hours, the long hours I have waited,
Pass from my thought, as I rest on thy bosom!

January 15, 1875.

SONG.

VOID of fragrance is the earth,
  Leafless, empty of delight;
Now is winter's biting mirth,
  And the wind is lord of night;
Far the moon spreads ceaselessly
Restless splendors on the sea.

What art thou, O fitful life,
  That in dewy roses bent;
Rustled in the maple's strife
  With the breeze that stole their scent;
Whose glad music broke on high
With the lark's song in the sky?

Art thou mortal, or dost hide
  In some covert dimly lit,
By no human eye descried,
  Though fair spirits walk in it?

All the heavens changeless are;
Art thou less than slightest star?

Come and break the icy brooks,
  Touch the grasses thin and dry,
Blossom in the forest nooks,
  Bid the new-fledged robins fly;
Frost and fever hold the earth
Till thou come with summer mirth.

Oh, the tender roseate dawn,
  Blooming o'er the quiet sea;
Oh, the perfumed lilies wan,
  Opening in the full-voiced glee
Of the thousand songsters gay,
With the first gleam of the day!

Oh, the wild delights of love
  That thou bringest in thy train,
When the white clouds melt above,
  And the heavens grow free from stain,
When the breeze sleeps on the sea,
And hushed is every rustling tree!

Fleeting is sweet life and frail:
  By us is no victory won.
Whirled on every dusty gale
  Are the generations gone.
Spirit, stay not, swiftly bring
Love and Beauty with the spring.

February 4, 1876.

MOODS.

WAKING this morn with happy heart
From a sweet dream of Paradise,
I flung my shutters wide apart:
The sun shone full across my eyes.

The birds beneath my window sat,
Carolled and twittered, loud and long:
Earth seemed so glad, and life so sweet,
My own lips, too, were filled with song.

. . . . . .

To-night my heart sinks in my breast, —
I fling my shutters wide again:
In clouds the sun sets in the west,
No rays slant up my window-pane.

The birds are in their nests asleep,
With drooping head and folded wing:
The darkness gathers fast and deep,
My lips are closed, I cannot sing.

February 5, 1875.

DESTINY.

"Sweet dream, a little longer stay." — *Clough.*

SWEET face I have seen but in dream,
  Shining out through my life like a star,
So tender and lovely you seem,
What must I believe that you are?

How weary and long are the days!
For me they are stripped of their charms:
I would fly from the sun's hated rays,
And be clasped once again in your arms.

Impatient with longing, I wait
Till the Future shall come with her wand,
For I know that you stand at the gate
Of the Eden that waits me beyond.

February 19, 1875.

LYDIAN AIRS.

"Lap me in soft Lydian airs." — MILTON'S *L'Allegro.*

I.

O ARABEL, awake!
Swiftly the day has sped;
Over a red-cloud lake,
In a golden boat she fled.
And now she 's sunk to rest far in the purpled west.

Take now thy tunêd lyre,
And sing a song for me;
My love is a tide of fire,
And it climbeth up to thee.
Through the close midnight give the lay whereby I live.

O Arabel, I come!
Thy music calleth me.

Let fade or flame the sun.
There 's naught in life but thee.
The fragrant white-thorn moves, and lends its
sweets to Love's.

II.

If any one fears death, he 's dead;
Joy's nectar flees from pallid lips.
If any one loves death, he 's mad;
Joy's nectar 's poison when he sips.

But if one minds not death at all,
He holdeth immortality;
Joy's nectar is his daily drink,
And all his nights pass jollily.

III.

In Daphne's groves at noon I came,
Escaping from the heat of life;
Through the cool glade shot sudden flame,
And filled my heart with turbid strife.
I cannot tell what chance befell,
As Aphrodite's languid spell,

Delirious with the joys of sense,
Hung o'er my will's enforced suspense,
Till, waking into ecstasy,
I heard a brook go murmuring by;
A bird that sang upon a spray
Of myrtle sweet smelt far away;
A breath whose sigh allured my eye
To gaze on works of fantasie,
As if of real mould were they.
Oh, that my gaze again might rest
On Beauty in her own light drest!
Oh, that my soul again might know
Ideal Beauty bodied so!
I cannot say what spell that day
Was on me; but I came away,
And in the night I wandered far
From where the groves of Daphne are.
And ever since, in loneliness,
I feed upon earth's ugliness,
And all my thoughts fore'er confess
The blessing of forgetfulness.

March 5, 1875.

TRANSLATIONS, PARAPHRASES, IMITATIONS.

HORACE. — ODES: I. 23.

YOU shun me, Chloë, like a hind
  That seeks its mother 'mid the mountain's mazes,
With foolish terrors at the wind,
  Or shady trees which rustle where she grazes.
For if the spring-time zephyrs make
  The branches wave, and leaflets murmuring quiver,
Or if green lizards stir the brake,
  Quick through its heart and knees there runs a shiver.
Yet I am not a tiger wild,
  Or Afric lion, you as prey pursuing.
Oh, cease, I beg you, like a child
  To keep your mother's side, when fit for wooing.

November 13, 1874.

HORACE. — ODES : III. 13.

O FOUNT of Bandusia, than crystal more clear,
Bright garlands are due thee with sweetest of wine;
To-morrow the kid, whose young horns just appear
From rough, shaggy brow, shall most gladly be thine.

His forehead, alas! has been swelling in vain;
For strife or for love he shall use it no more;
But — a wanton herd's son as he is — he shall stain,
In honor of thee, thy cold streamlets with gore.

Thy streamlets, — they know not Canicula's fire,
The fierce, burning heat when its season is nigh;

Ah, no! thou refreshest the oxen which tire
  Of the plough; thou refreshest the herd passing by.

Some fountains the greatest of glories have known;
  Thou too, when I sing, shalt seem worthy renown;
When I sing of the oak that is shading the stone
  From whose heart thy clear water leaps prattlingly down.

May 28, 1875.

VERG.—ECL. VII.

56–60.

THE woodlands brown are parched with heat,
The grasses wither at our feet;
Upon the hills the God of Wine
No longer guards the tender vine.
Yet, when my darling's face is seen,
The grass will bloom in living green,
And softly from the clouds will fall
The showers that cheer the hearts of all.

61–64.

Alcides keeps the poplar grove,
The purpling grape is Bacchus' love;
Fair Venus on the myrtle breathes,
Apollo's locks the laurel wreathes.

But Phillis loves the hazel-trees,
And, if she still shall cherish these,
Nor laurel shall with these compare,
Nor myrtle twined in Venus' hair.

June 11, 1875.

CATULLUS. — CARM. V.

LET us live and love, dear girl,
  Ere the evil days draw nigh,
Heeding not our sires' reproving:
Did not they grow old in loving?
We'll be preachers by and by, —
You a prude, and I a churl.

Suns that here have had their setting
May again describe their courses;
But, when our brief life is over,
It is past beyond recover.
Bear us then, Death's sable horses,
Down to sleep and sad forgetting.

Give me, sweet, a thousand kisses,
Then a hundred, and repeat them;
Let them fall on me like showers,
Fresh as dew at twilight hours.

Let my own go forth to meet them:
What reck we amid such blisses?

But these thousands higher mounting,
We must stop; and, ere we slumber,
So confuse and intersperse them,
Intermingle and reverse them,
That no one can tell the number,
Nor grow envious at the counting.

January 9, 1874.

CATULLUS.

IMITATION OF CARM. LXX.

MY sweetheart vows to wed me true
Though all the world should come to woo:
Nay, e'en, if, other swains apart,
Great Jove himself should ask her heart,
She would refuse him for my sake.
She vows, — but vows fair women make,
And tender words sweet girls repeat
To lovers kneeling at their feet,
Breathe to the winds that whisper nigh,
Or write in brooks that hasten by.

February 6, 1874.

TIBULLUS. — LIB. III. ELEG. 13.

IMITATION.

NO maid from thee shall win my heart,
Or pluck with lily hand apart
Those threads of gold the Queen of Love
In silken meshes round us wove,
When first our eyes and warm lips met.
Thy face alone can charm me yet.
Through all the town mine eyes can see
None other beautiful but thee.
And I could wish — but, ah! how vain —
That all beside might call thee plain;
For then my heart were free from care,
If thou to me alone wert fair.
Seek not from other lips thy praise,
But shun, sweet maid, the vulgar gaze.
They wisely love who deem the best
Those charms whose sight no eyes have blest.
Thus would my days with thee be sweet,
In wilds untrod by human feet;
Thy presence in the lonely wood
Would fill with life the solitude.

For thou art rest from cares, my light
When dark about me broods the night.
Now, though to me a maiden sent
From heaven her footsteps earthward bent,
'T were vain: yea, e'en though Venus came,
She could not set my heart aflame.
To thee my deathless love I vow
In Juno's sacred name, who now
Shall be my goddess for thy sake.
Mad youth, what have I done? Why take
Upon my lips that foolish oath?
Alas! henceforth, however loath,
I cannot break the vow I made.
My very fear has all betrayed.
Now thou wilt cold and cruel turn;
My heart with fires intenser burn.
My thoughtless tongue has wrought this ill;
But I obey thine own sweet will,
And ever true to thee remain,
Nor seek to break my weary chain.
Now fettered to the shrine I steal,
And low before dear Venus kneel;
Who loads the base with endless cares,
But listens to the lover's prayers.

February 20, 1874.

ARISTOPHANES. — BIRDS.

VV. 211–226.

ARISE, arise, my mate, and cease thy sleeping;
I pray thee chaunt the strain of hymns divine,
Which from thy heavenly throat thou utt'rest; weeping
For much-lamented Itys, mine and thine.

Thy golden beak the flowing measure trills,
And echo, clear-resounding, upward flies, —
Upward from leafy yew to where it fills
The heavenly homes, the temples in the skies.

Then golden-haired Apollo hears the strain
Of thy most mournful dirge, and with his lyre,
Ivory-decked, responds to the refrain,
And leads the dances of the heavenly choir.

Then from the throats of those that never die
  Harmonious sounds in unison are heard,
Divinely blest, a wailing melody.
  (And now they hear the piping of a bird.)

May 14, 1875

PARAPHRASES ON HEINE.

I.

A LONELY Pine-tree riseth
  Against the sky gray cold,
And, while he sleeps, his branches
  The ice and snow enfold.

He dreams of one fair Palm-tree.
  In lands of morning light;
And, waking, moans in silence
  Upon his rocky height.

II.

If I but hear it ringing, —
  The song that long ago
I heard my lady singing, —
  My breast is thrilled with woe.

Love-longing drives me lonely,
  Where nought my grieving hears,

And in the dark wood only
  Forgets itself in tears.

III.

This happy summer morning
  I in my garden walk,
And silent hear the blossoms
  In whispered accents talk.

They pity me, and whisper
  Such comfort as they can:
"Our sister is too cruel,
  O pale, unhappy man!"

IV.

When I but gaze into thine eyes,
Then flies my grief, my sorrow flies;
And when I kiss thy lips, my heart
In health new found forgets its smart.

When I upon thy bosom rest,
The bliss of heaven steals through my breast;
And when thou say'st, "I love but thee,"
I weep, unwilling, bitterly.

V.

Oh, lay thy cheek by mine, since tears
  Adown them both are flowing;
And press thy heart more close to mine,
  Since both with flames are glowing.

And when upon those flames shall flow
  The tear-drops thickly thronging,
Around thee I my arm will throw,
  And die of sweet love-longing.

April 2, 1875.

SONNETS.

DOLCE FAR NIENTE.

DOWN on the grass beneath a tree I lay, —
'T was one of Lowell's rarest "days in June" —
To enjoy the long, rich summer afternoon.
I saw the heat uprising from the hay,
And heard from far, upon his busy way,
A bumble-bee, come booming onward; soon
His hum was lost amid the quiet tune
Which all the fields sing on a summer's day.
The reeds within the brook moved to and fro;
Close by, a pickerel jumped and caught a fly;
Above, the cumulated clouds moved slow,
So slow the motions scarce could catch the eye.
O'erhead a breath of wind was rustling low,
And made the leaves just gossip dreamily.

December 23, 1868.

A CHILD.

OFT as a child I played amid the sand,
  And built me castles on the shingly beach;
  For their foundations, gathering from the reach
Of playful wavelets, in my eager hand,
The smooth, white pebbles thick upon the strand:
  While rose successive in the morning sun
  Visions that charmed an hour, then, one by one,
Like magic palaces of fairy-land,
  Melted away before my longing sight.
Now childhood too has gone, and I have smiled
  At times to think how brief was its delight.
And yet, methinks, my heart is still beguiled
  By unsubstantial dreams, as brief and bright
As those of old, — and I am still a child.

October 3, 1873.

BY NIGHT.

MY lamp is out; and at the open pane
I stand, and gaze into the sobbing night.
Upon the roof above me pats the rain;
And the chill, gusty wind, as if in fright,
Comes shrieking by. Below I see the light
Flickering on the melancholy street;
And, like a gliding shadow, comes in sight
The dripping watchman on his lonely beat.
But now a strange, weird light through rifts of cloud
Is breaking, and the mist drives fast above;
And now sad earth is once again endowed
With the sweet glances of the queen of love.
And so it is the clouds of my despair
Are oft dispelled by smiles from thee, my fair!

January 23, 1874.

AN EASTER SUNRISE.

THINK how the sun doth rise upon this morn!
Immortals wear not immortality
More grandly on their perfect brows than He
Now lifts his orbèd splendors o'er the dawn.
Oh! multitudinous bounty of him born!
Think how the stellar spaces ceaselessly
Shake with the speed of his great charity,
That rolls its golden floods all worlds along.
O gathered glory of the universe,
Shame blushes through my being's whitest soul
For my hands scant of gifts, and heart — oh, worse!
Ungenerous of love, profuse of dole;
O thou who dost all mercies free disburse,
My great example be, my single goal.

April 16, 1875.

THEE.

THE light of thy sweet face forever shines
Bright as the sun above my path, perplexed
With fear and doubt, and oft with thistles vexed.
The thought of thee with every thought entwines,
And in each changing cloud my heart divines
Some message from thy lips. Whate'er the text
I chance to read, I lose the meaning, next
The words, but see thy name between the lines.
Yet though my heart is bound to thee so fast,
For such sweet servitude I cannot grieve:
Nay, though a single touch of mine would cast
My chains aside, those chains I would not leave;
But pray my bondage might forever last,
Whilst I song-chaplets for thy brow might weave.

October 16, 1874.

TO THE STATUE OF BEETHOVEN IN THE MUSIC HALL.

WITH downcast brow, as wrapt in musings grand,
Thou standest ever, through the lonely night,
Or when the hall, through all its listening height,
Echoes thy music from some master hand.
O wondrous heaven-taught spirit, who hast planned
These magic-woven harmonies aright
To hold us spell-bound in a strange delight,
While each emotion starts at thy command,
Cannot the subtle language of thine art
Waft us some message from the silent shore
Thrilling the depths of every world-worn heart?
A childish longing! Thou hast told before
What we, at best, interpret but in part:
We could not understand thee telling more.

December 9, 1870.

FRA ANGELICO.

I LIKE the story of that monk who knelt
In prayer devout, and, lest some thought of sin
Should mar its grace, dared not his work begin
Till in the silence of his heart he felt
Thought grow divine and earthly longings melt
Beneath God's touch, and o'er the Babel din
Heard the clear whisper of the Christ within.
What wonder, when such inspiration dwelt
In his calm bosom, that he dared not rise,
But day by day, with meek and lowly heart,
Painted upon his bended knees, and wise
Deemed not the work his own, but his the part
To seize what God revealed unto his eyes,
And bid the panel glow with holy art!

May 29, 1874.

PERICLES.

HIS grave, impassive face was stern and cold;
Upon his brow majestic calmness sate;
The fine curve of his lips, as firm as fate,
Of deep resolve and fast persuasion told.
No features, his, of coarse and common mould,
But, first of men in the world's foremost state,
Even at her highest, he, among the great,
Excelled by brow and breast the men of old.
And unto us who, through the night of years,
See men like shadows move along the dim
Horizon's verge, high o'er them all appears,
Clearer than all beside, the shape of him
Who gave his name to Athens' noblest age,
Whose life gave history her brightest page.

March 19, 1875.

SUMNER.

THE fire is dead. The altar stones are cold.
No more rich clouds of incense heaven-ward rise.
Untouched upon the coals the censer lies,
That fragrant swung unceasingly of old:
No hands impure may touch that hallowed gold.
Detained no more by gift or sacrifice,
The goddess seeks again her native skies.
And yet no blazing portals have foretold
Her passage to the stars, and street and mart
Know not that from the shrine her feet have fled.
But Freedom's great High Priest, who set apart
His life, while others sought but gold or bread,
To guard her sacred fire, thrice noble heart!
Lies in her silent temple, cold and dead.

March 20, 1874.

TO J.

I ONLY saw you once; but then mine eyes,
Not pure, alas! brought you to gaze on me.
You shared my sin: I shared your purity.
I felt a nobler life in me arise:
You felt sin enter at your pure heart's door.
That sin was changed when in so sweet a place;
And, stronger in its nature, with new grace
Your innocence was greater than before.
And then we hesitated; though we knew
Each other's souls, yet custom threw her chains
About us, and far from each other drew
Two hearts that felt each other's joys and pains.
Seen once, I left you. Ah! if e'er seen more,
How could I know you better than before?

April 27, 1867.

WORSHIP.

THE praises Nature utters never fail.
The lark's loud matin brings the noon-day hymn
Of throstles, lost, in turn, amid the dim
Aisles of the twilight world; while through the vale
The sad, sweet vespers of the nightingale
Through leafy arches to the skies ascend.
Nor does the worship of her full heart end
In praise alone; but, day by day, those pale
White lilies breathe an air of sacred hope,
And night by night, beneath the summer sky,
The blue-eyed violets on every slope
Shame our weak faith; and fervent charity
Is in the May-flower's perfume. Thus earth's days
Are full of silent prayer and sweetest praise.

October 1, 1874.

SHELLEY.

"And Shelley with his white ideal
All statue-blind."

WHO hath not felt, while gazing on the fair,
Eternal stars that roam the azure deep,
The shadows of a vaster being sweep
Over his darkling soul, and all the air
Grow murmurous with motions of swift wings,
Mighty, innumerable, unrevealed,
Whispering dim prophecies of things concealed
Beyond the scope of our imaginings?
O poet, thus thy thoughts o'ershadow me!
A wingèd wonder watching o'er my heart,
Prompting sweet visions and bright hopes, that dart
Like radiant rainbows o'er the clouds of doubt,
Or flash like new-born worlds from out the dark,
Bright guiders homeward of my tossing bark.

February 20, 1874.

UNNOTICED LOVE.

IF any soul grows faint in loving one
Who knoweth not his spirit's brooding care,
Whose cup, o'erbrimmed with grosser wines, doth spare
That love's bright, red-heart vintage should outrun
And lose its precious liquids in the sun,
Let him love's utmost charity outdare,
And all his resolute energies upbear
To where love knoweth not if love be won.
Let him find ceaseless joy, be glad at heart,
That there is *one* with whom he may commune,
Though scantly, and at moments far apart,—
Whose life he may by glimpses e'en illume;
One ray is strong to save, as all that dart
From the unshaded splendors of the noon.

April 16, 1875.

FAITHFULNESS.

"Sole as the turtle that hath lost her make." — *Chaucer.*

THE turtle-dove whose soft-eyed mate is dead
Seeks for none other with her downy breast
To cheer the darkness of his lonely nest,
But broods in sorrow o'er the lost instead.
Her eyes whose love-light once his own eyes fed
Stole away all the beauty from the rest;
None else can charm him who has known the best,
Nor will the mourning mate another wed.
And if but one can fill the love of bird,
Think'st thou my heart shall more forgetful be?
When once thy sweetest accents I have heard,
Another's voice can sound as sweet to me?
Ah, no! till love be an unmeaning word,
True as the dove, I ever cling to thee!

May 6, 1874.

BY THE NIGHT SEA.

WHERE stalwart pines o'erhang a craggy sea,
Their sombre shadows rocking on the surf,
Star-hushed, I lie upon the scanty turf,
Silent in a slow-thoughted revery.
The still, grand moon rises triumphantly,
And hoary ocean at her golden birth
Smiles like a young Endymion, while the earth
From her broad meadows breathes low melody.
O what a calméd wonder overskies
The heart grown still with looking on the waves,
Where the eternity of beauty lies!
Throned on the softened waters Dian laves,
And ceaselessly upon the night arise
Ten thousand echoes from harmonious caves.

November 27, 1874.

THE SMITHY.

THICK fell the starry flakes of glistening snow,
And now the drifting sleet is pelting past;
It beats against the window, freezing fast,
And the rude winds through creaking branches blow.
But, in the smithy bright, the embers glow
With cheerful light, and flickering shadows cast.
A knot of townsfolk, driven by the blast,
Seek a snug refuge 'neath the rafters low,
And gossip o'er the matters of the day.
Patient the faithful, weary horses stand,
And, like their masters, gladly would they stay;
But forth into the cold must plod their way,
Dragging the wood-sledge, piled by thrifty hand,
To make with blazing fire the cottage gay.

January 31, 1873.

www.ingramcontent.com/pod-product-compliance
Lightning Source LLC
LaVergne TN
LVHW010248110826
845151LV00004B/1418

* 9 7 8 1 4 2 5 5 2 4 7 6 0 *